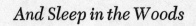

And Sleep in the Woods

Also by Thomas York

WE, THE WILDERNESS
SNOWMAN

And Sleep in the Woods

The Story of
One Man's Spiritual Quest

THOMAS YORK

1978

Doubleday Canada Limited, Toronto, Ontario
Doubleday & Company, Inc., Garden City, New York

Library of Congress Cataloging in Publication Data
York, Thomas Lee.
And Sleep in the Woods.
1. York, Thomas Lee. 2. Converts—Canada—
Biography. 3. Vietnamese Conflict,
1961–1975—Draft resisters—Arkansas. I. Title.
BV4935.Y67A32   248'.2'0924 [B]
ISBN: 0-385-13236-0
Library of Congress Catalog Card Number 77–82775

For Paul, Stephen, Rachel, and Sarah.

Author's Note

The beginning and end came to me in a dream. I recorded the dream (how I fell asleep walking into a painting, and woke up walking out of a trial), and the intervening story wrote itself. Except for the frame device, however, all the rest of the story is true. Everything happened as I have recorded, and none of the names has been changed.

Only once I was tempted to alter a name; but John Smith seemed a name to change to, not from. And since Rev. Smith is portrayed as representative of the conservative ministry as it is, I left his name as it was.

The material in the last section relating to the minister in Little Rock appeared first in slightly different form in the *Christian Century* (August 2, 1972), under the title "Get Out of Town!" It provoked adverse response, and was reprinted in the Vancouver *Sun* (October 18, 1972), where it elicited the opposite response.

The trial sequences in the last section are taken from the federal district court transcript, available in the published form required by a United States court of appeals. Since the full transcript runs to nearly two hundred pages, I have selected only a few passages to indicate the atmosphere of the trial. It did not seem appropriate there, as it does here, to express appreciation to my two lawyers, Messrs. Gitchell and Cearly, or to vilify the government's attorney, Mr. Riddick. Lawyers, like ministers, are subject to irrational responses simply because they are lawyers; but I was fortunate to find two who believed in my case, and who did not press me for money. The judge, I think, speaks for himself.

I began with a dream, and awoke to a nightmare. I set out to chronicle a sleep in the woods, and found myself battling a dragon. I do not flatter myself that this book will be considered anything other than presumptuous and peevish—the musings of a mystical and paranoid mind; for I have long since awakened from that dream I once had, while asleep and at peace in the woods, of a nation not imprisoned, and a house not divided.

Contents

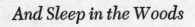

And Sleep in the Woods

DRAGONS AND DAYDREAMS

One

I am waiting for Stephen, our six-year-old middle child,
while he takes his time selecting a Yo-Yo in the new shop-
ping plaza. I sit in the car outside, its engine throbbing into
the thickness of a drizzly September evening. Shadowy
figures, sliced by my headlights and those of a thousand
other cars, throng between the parking lot and the mall. All
around me loom high-rises—the tallest forty-four stories, the
one I live in half that tall—monoliths rising out of the mist
like the remnants of some ancient religion whose significance has been lost. Across the mall, though I can scarcely
see its outline, stands the church; in front of the church,
though I can't see it at all, stands a sign announcing the
hours of Catholic Mass and Protestant worship, with the
names in smaller letters of the RC priest, and the United
Church minister—me.

For all its familiarity, this mall in suburban Toronto might
be mistaken for any of a hundred others, the high-rises

around it for apartment complexes in a thousand other cities. In spite of the knowledge that I live here, and that it is here I belong, I do not—this autumn evening of low visibility—feel very secure. The cars on the lot, my own included, smoke and groan and idle and throb like so many dinosaurs yarded together. Mothers inside the mall thrust and jostle around counters of goods they do not need. Fathers wait in cars or rifle through raw meats in the supermarket while their wives accost lingerie. All have been drawn in —from Europe, from Asia, from small farms in Ontario and small towns in upstate New York—into the civilized combat: with whom? and for what? The darkened presence of the church within the druidical ring of high-rises assures me that we are on the right side, though it is not the side that wins. The winning side is chaos and unreason—the cold, the wet, and the dark. But in the face of oncoming darkness, our defeat is no refutation.

Meanwhile, I wait. And since I was waiting anyway, I thought I might as well turn off the engine and walk in and browse around. It was, after all, a "grand opening." There might be some bargains on dresses for Rachel, our five-year-old; or some art supplies for Paul, who is eight. If only the crowds weren't too dense . . . I didn't want to miss Stephen, and I did want to get home. . . .

I found myself, after first fronting the crowd and then giving way and letting it steer me, shunted in through the door of an art gallery that was strangely devoid of people—a new store, just opened, with yellow-pile carpet swathing a spacious area. I breathed easily. Not only was the single large room uncluttered by bric-a-brac, but there was not here the throbbing urgence to rummage and purchase that I had felt in passing Teen Jeans, or in being pushed through Woolco, where the densest crowd milled. Two paintings at one end of the wide room dominated the gallery. Both were large, though the one on the left, which I would estimate as about ten feet high by twenty feet wide, was larger than the other, which was approximately eight feet by fourteen feet. Both rested their foregrounds on the carpeted floor and reached nearly to the ceiling, supported, presumably, by a network of easels and wires. Both were framed, but without glass and not permanently, for there were folds and wrinkles in each. They portrayed the following scenes: a sea of browned lawn-grass occupied most of one side of each panel, to a height of about six feet; with perhaps four feet of pale sky above. The left side of each was filled by a flat southern mansion, exceedingly white and well-kept, complete with porticos and proto-Dorian pillars. The whole façade had a statuesque quality—the vivid sense of life once removed, which memory sometimes elicits—as though the mansions portrayed were complete in themselves, yet devoid of life.

I stood in the center of the wide room and stared at the one, then at the other, canvas; the two, while not identical, were similar. The larger, the one on the left, bore in one corner a signature, "Thom," and was priced with a square of white paper attached to the frame, "$7—." (I couldn't distinguish the last three numbers, but the price was above seven thousand dollars.) The larger painting, now that I tried to account for its price, did look as though it were an original, while the smaller was definitely a print, its surface glossy and smooth. While I stood appraising, oblivious of my surroundings, the lady who kept the shop came up behind me; I had noticed the price of the one and was searching for a price on the other when I became aware of her at my elbow. Without glancing away from the paintings, I asked her if the larger painting by "Thom" (I slurred the name, uncertain of how to pronounce it) was an original. "Oh no," she said, "the scene by Thom, or Hom—it's a reproduction." And while she was still talking, and I still gazing at the huge canvas, which for all she said to the contrary looked original to me, I seemed without moving physically toward it to be progressively absorbed into it . . . and found myself, not indeed in the porticoed mansion portrayed, but walking with Lynn by my side up a dusty red road toward an old southern mansion far less ideal, to be sure, but stylistically much like the one in Thom's painting. . . .

The house we lived in that winter, that winter we lived disguised to ourselves and to the world as students and as newlyweds, was a dilapidated manor on a disused five-hundred-acre plantation. You found it, Lynn, and rented it from the realtor for fifty dollars a month. Besides the main house—two stories, nine rooms without heat, except for the huge fireplace in the kitchen—there was the ramshackle barn (which we rented, in turn, to the fraternities at Duke and the University of North Carolina for their parties), a pumphouse, an orchard, a garden plot, and several slave quarters of stone, with dirt floors and without windows, located on the northeastern, the southeastern, and the southwestern quarters of the vast tract. The property was cut, about a quarter mile south of the house, by a deep wooded ravine, which I robbed of wolf trees that winter. In the frosty North Carolina mornings, my ax on my shoulder, I would disappear into the gloom of the ravine. The mold of dead leaves would be sodden, the trees silent; often I was rewarded with a glimpse of a deer, and always by the spectacle of an opossum hanging from a persimmon tree, or scrabbling for fruit at its base. By the time the slugabed sun found me out and opened his eyes on my work, I was already sweating and hauling the hickory stumps and cypress roots and pine knots up the defile. The hill was steep, and the leaves slick, and I muttered and cursed and fell and got muddy, but it didn't matter: you were always there, Lynn, when I brought the wood in; you had the dew upon you, and breakfast ready.

There was a two-acre pond a half mile or so behind the house, and beyond that a vast swamp into which the ravine drained. This swamp on whose edge we lived we nicknamed the "Great Dismal," but left unexplored; the pond, though, we frequented daily.

It was a deep pond, bounded on the far side by a railroad embankment, which separated it, so far as the eye could see, from the Great Dismal beyond. But beneath the track, and through the levee deeper down, there must have been seepage, for all sorts of antediluvian creatures—frogs, snakes, and turtles—found their way into the pond, and fish with which the pond had been stocked found their way out to the swamp. I fished that pond, gigged frogs there, and speared water moccasins. Come spring, while you worked your garden, nude, beneath the strong young sun, I would run barefoot down the path to the pond, leap lively in, swim the length a few times, then float on my back. There was always such a scent of crushed mint; to get to the pond one had to tread on a bank of wild flowers, and the slightest breeze, when one lay on his back, wafted the freshness of mint. Then as I lay in the water looking up at the sky, hearing the chirrup of crickets and inhaling the greenness of mint, having come from you and having you to go back to—then I might have known bliss and contentment, even on the Great Dismal's edge, had my pleasant surroundings found response from a peace within.

But I was mad and violent and driven, discontent and, as much as could be permitted in that plantation setting, crazed. The Sunday the blacks from down the track dredged up the seventy-five-pound turtle with three legs, I saw in its clumsy scramblings my own efforts to evade the draft; my dull presence at graduate school, which kept me exempt; and intimations of the Great Dismal beyond.

When then you dropped out of graduate school and started teaching to support us and to keep me enrolled, my rambles took me more and more often to the deserted slave quarters and past the pond to the edge of the swamp. I would pace the railroad track that bounded the unworked plantation, a prey to depressions for which I hadn't images yet. Only an elderly turtle who had lost one leg in a trap, a ramshackle cotton plantation due soon to be subdivided, and, stretching southward as far as I could imagine, the Great Dismal.

Two

The last time I saw my father was that summer before we left for Canada. Canada had never entered our minds, much less our plans, and I left you working your garden, Lynn—string beans we would not be around to harvest, squash we would never eat—while I took the long bus trip to Little Rock.

All across North Carolina, and then Tennessee, the countryside had a drawn and withered look, as if good had gone underground, and the doubtful been banished. A hundred miles farther south, though I didn't know it then, a coalition of liberals and blacks under the leadership of Martin Luther King, Jr., was preparing to march over much the same ground that Sherman had covered nearly a century earlier. And JFK, midway through his second year as President, was busy implementing the Supreme Court's desegregation pronouncement, while launching his own space program. It was to be a pyrotechnic decade for America—replete with Woodstocks, moon shots, and assassinations—but of such things I, like everyone else, was unaware. Crossing by bus the Smoky Mountains of North Carolina and the clay hills of Tennessee, rethinking my master's thesis ("The Concept of Morale in the Allied Bombing of Germany in World War II"), which had been returned for corrections, I didn't stop off at your parents' place, Lynn, and in those days they would have received me. Not that they were pleased that we had eloped, but your father had retired from the Joint Chiefs of Staff, and he and I could have sat on the veranda of the aerie he had built in the Smokies and, in the best southern tradition, sipped liqueurs while smoking cigars and discussed his part in the bombing of cities.

But I didn't stop off, being even then driven, slantwise, against the South's grain, and too preoccupied with the world's past to attend to your father's. I fancied then, though it seems trite now, that the universe impinged on each individual, and at the point of greatest pressure either broke him or drove a way through him to his, and its own, fulfillment. That was why I'd chosen the bombing topic—because I'd served a summer aboard an aircraft carrier, and despised the military; that was why I'd enrolled in graduate school—because I'd gone AWOL from my college NROTC unit, and was high on the draftable list; and that was why, no doubt, I was traveling west before doing anything rash—because my father, whom I had not seen in over a year and was never to see again, was a lawyer and might be able to help me.

I can picture him now as I found him that summer, the summer of '62: already sick but concealing it, sitting at his desk in the Little Rock office at the rear of the restaurant on Cantrell Road, the office he'd moved to after the affair of Faubus' income tax. Earlier, at the height of the Little Rock faceoff over school desegregation, my father, who had been with the IRS for twenty years, was scapegoated over an error in the governor's tax assessment. Whereupon my father had been demoted and transferred—to Dallas, from which he commuted on weekends!—and had then resigned, or retired, and opened his own law practice. His clients, since he refused to take divorce cases, included a Mexican radio preacher (the same who buried him); a rainmaker who worked from the back of a truck mainly in Oklahoma; Sam Jones, the state land commissioner (who was constantly buying and selling land on the side, and whose office was staffed with old girlfriends); and Q. Byrum Hurst, a state senator (who subsequently spent two years in the state penitentiary on conviction of graft). No, cases were not going swimmingly for my father, who had chosen to launch his legal career at age fifty.

My father—I can still see him sitting calmly alone in his office at the end of the corridor, a quiet presence, once a fine athlete (in football he played center for Navy in '29, and in golf he beat Bobby Jones), now a sick man . . . burst in upon by his volatile son, intent on haranguing him about *my* condition, *my* status, *my* future—"My son, my son"—mustering his energies, even though he was sick, to try to persuade me of the foolhardiness of quitting graduate school, and the even greater madness of bucking the draft—a quiet, peaceable, mystical man, a broken man—my father: "Not only will they not let you get away with it, but they'll hound you wherever you go and for the rest of your life."

"Not if I go to Canada, and Canada doesn't extradite."

"And what will you do in Canada? And where will Lynn be all this time?"

"I'll trap, and Lynn will be with me. We'll do whatever's necessary."

"You'll go to Canada, and you'll trap. Then you're a bigger fool than I thought. Why, you've never even seen snow, and you know nothing at all about trapping. Your

grandparents came from Canada because there were no potatoes, and cleaned latrines and caught lobsters in Maine so
that I could finish high school. And when I met and married
your mother, quick as a flash we came here to Arkansas,
where her people at least had some property, and you didn't
have to shovel your way to the road, and freeze your feet
walking to school. Now you're traipsing off to Canada and
dragging Lynn along too. Have you told her? What does she
think about it? All because you're afraid of two years, two
years in the Army."

"It's not just that; it's not just the two years."

"What is it then?"

"It's that I can see the end here, before I've even begun.
You probably felt the same about Maine, except there it was
the hardship, here it's the prosperity. There's a prefab pattern that I can't see myself fitting into—it's not the South, it's
just me—that I'd sooner commit suicide than conform to. But
North, for some reason the North allures me—the snow, the
bush, the spaciousness—all those things. . . . Of course, I
don't know what I'll do when I get there, that's why I want
to go; and I really think I must go to find out. Maybe it will
prove difficult, maybe too difficult, but—well, we'll see. . . ."

My father had strongly urged me to heed his counsel on
only one other occasion ("Don't go to a northern college,"
he'd said when I got the NROTC scholarship, "it'll make a
snob of you. Why not go to Tulane?" And to Tulane I had
gone, and met Lynn, and got married). My father, who
himself had dropped out of Annapolis to get married, and
who understood though he didn't condone such mad pranks,
rose heavily to his feet and looked at me, then came around
from behind his desk and bear-hugged me. I took this
clumsy caress, since he was not a demonstrative man, as his
blessing on my woodward urge. But now I know better: it
was his farewell.

Later that evening, so my mother tells me, he said: "I'm

afraid Tom is selfish. He has this wild scheme of going with Lynn to Canada, to avoid the draft. I tried to tell him that it would be difficult for him there, and even more difficult for him here when he returns. Of course, it's unthinkable that he should stay there; that anyone does is a wonder. I only hope he doesn't insist on finding that out for himself, and on dragging poor Lynn along with him."

To which my mother—speaking to my father ("Duke") but gazing at the portrait of her dead sire ("Poppa"), which dominated the sitting room of my grandmother's house—my mother might have replied: "Poppa always wanted to try Canada. He said there was a fortune to be made there in timber. If only he had lived a little longer, he might have gone North and made a start for Tom."

At which my father may have thought: "Yes, your father might have gone—on horseback, of course, with his gang of black men to slave for him, and black women to serve him—and left your mother here in Little Rock for me to look after." But if he thought it, he didn't say it. He only said, "Tom's selfish, there's no denying that, but he's young yet. Maybe he'll grow out of it before he does something rash, or maybe Lynn can restrain him. I hope so."

Three

In the fall of that year, 1962, on my twenty-second birthday, Lynn, you nearly killed yourself. You were driving the old Ford my father had given us, speeding along the forty miles of country road you commuted every morning to school-teach, when a car pulled out in front of you from a blind intersection—he was going about forty miles per hour, you about sixty miles per hour—and you plowed into him, catapulted through the air, and landed right-side-up in a farmer's field. When then you ran the hundred yards to where his car had landed, when you pried open his driver's door and saw the crumpled man, the blood, and that he had no legs—did you confront the horror then, the transience of human existence? Or did you quail, your legs still pumping, feet still stamping the astonished earth . . . before the man, seeing in your wide-eyed stare and gaping O of mouth such shock, and seeing that you thought yourself responsible, managed with his hand to indicate the pull brakes and equipage of a legless person's car?

You continued on to school and taught that day, as I remember, until you fainted, still in shock, and had to be brought home. But whether or not the accident had anything to do with what then seemed our sudden decision to depart for Canada, the insurance settlement secured for us the truck in which we came.

It was a Chevy pickup, with an oversized bed, which we nicknamed "Big Horse." We used it first at the community hog slaughter. I can still remember driving to the neighboring farm on a frosty November morning, the garden plots all brown and crushed except for globes of pumpkins, the smell of mowed hay in the air, the chill of frost, advent of winter. And then, in that back-country hollow, where harvest and slaughter-time fell with the sun and without reference to Thanksgiving or Christmas, sighting in their sty below the barn the gorged and grunting victims—six shoats and an aged sow—rooting and snuffling for swill. When they were led one by one through the jerry-built chute, strung up suddenly by the hind legs on a singletree attached to a block and tackle, and their throats slit, each one groaned and kicked, but they were too fat and too much in man's power to protest long or to slow the proceedings. With hearts still pumping and throats still bleeding, they were swung on their singletree clear of the chute and lowered head first into the hot water tank, scalded, scraped (the bristles set by for brushes), raised again and their bellies slit while the mass of guts that slid out was caught in waiting wheelbarrows and carted up the hill. There in the several outbuildings where black women, aided by pickaninnies, sat majestically sweating and surrounded by flies, the various by-products were processed—into chitterlings, pig's feet, hog jowls, pork liver, kidneys, lights, tripe, and the beginnings of sausage—each woman as the wheelbarrow came by reaching in, drawing out, and with a quick slash of her knife severing the ingredients needful to her—there were, in all, fourteen such stations —while the men, left outside with the carcasses, quartered and then butchered them.

I helped that day with the butchering, and the experience of it stood me in good stead later on; while you, Lynn, looked on and said you couldn't quite stomach the drawing and pressing and turning inside out and then stuffing of long strings of guts involved in the making of chitterlings. But mainly Big Horse was employed in delivering meat to the various farms, and for that we took home fresh ham.

Oh the smoking, steaming, acrid, and organic-smelling imprint of that day! Long afterward I remembered and regarded hog slaughter and pumpkin harvest in the South as the stay-at-home brother's legacy from which we had fled to another country, for we had neither stocks of food, nor winter clothes, nor a permanent shelter, nor a job awaiting us, nor money; and there were times when we would have eaten chitterlings gladly, had we only the ingredients to make them; for certainly we fled precipitately, and with as little forethought as any fugitive. And, to add to our discomfort, our flight was in winter. Having packed in haste and driven nonstop from North Carolina through the border states of Virginia and West Virginia, then through the northern states of Pennsylvania and New York, where we first encountered snow and ice, we crossed the border at Fort Erie, Ontario, at midnight on December 28, 1962.

We entered Canada as "landed immigrants," with a truckload of junk—household appliances, a broom, a bed, a typewriter—whatever would fit into Big Horse, you insisted on bringing, Lynn. The customs official sleepily untied one corner of the tarpaulin, flashed his light in, marked "negligible" under "Belongings," and waved us through. We came as thousands of other immigrants had come and would come (though few, as yet, from the United States—this was before

Vietnam), but no two immigrants ever landed with greater urgency, or keener instinct for survival, or surer expectation of hardship. We had the smell of fear about us, and the aspect of flight. Behind us was the feeding trough, which we associated with slaughter; ahead, the land of struggle and freedom, land without fences, land of snow. Like other unprepared, ill-informed Southerners we expected to be met at the border by Eskimos, and to be taught to live off the land. Imagine our surprise, then, on approaching Toronto via Highway 401, a city larger than any we had bypassed en route, and so foreboding under its sheet of industrial snow that we bypassed it too, and kept trundling on toward Ottawa.

All along the way (after we left the highway and took to the side roads), through small rural town after town separated by mile upon mile of snow-smooth concession blocks backed by dark borders of forest and fronted by drifted snowbanks, all along the way we kept stopping—to stand beside the truck beneath the snow-laden sky and gaze northward across the smooth fields to the shadowy outlines of trees, themselves bounded by other, further horizons. It wasn't the lure of cities that had brought us this far, but of country, and beyond that more country, and beyond that, wilderness—as if the vague haze of trees on the horizon were a hand in the webwork of spirit beckoning us on, and we cutting crosslots and cattycorner to be brushed by that dark angel's wing. But without winter clothes, and coming straight from the South, as we stood on the snow-blown roadside peering northward into the distance, the tops of our heads felt fair to bursting, like pumpkins swollen with frost. We were hungry, too, and tired, and our money nearly all gone; but mainly we were cold—so we continued on to Ottawa.

There we found an apartment and secured jobs, you showing "model" apartments in a new building, I as a reporter on the Ottawa *Citizen*. We bought fur-lined boots and wool toques and gloves (but made do with our old coats worn over several sweaters), and walked snowy streets arm in arm to keep warm while our breaths frosted together. We watched children equipped with ice skates and curved sticks play a curious game on outdoor ice rinks, and firemen fight flames with water that froze as soon as it struck the building. We lived in a sleazy tenement, which was all we could afford, and from which within a month of our coming I wrote my draft board in Little Rock:

February 10, 1963

Dear Board:

This is to inform you that the undersigned, formerly a student at Duke University, Durham, North Carolina, did on the 28th day of December, 1962, enter Canada as a "landed immigrant," he and his wife passing through the port of entry at Fort Erie, Ontario, en route to their permanent residence at 508 Besserer St., Ottawa, Ontario. It is their intention to reside permanently at that address, and in five years to become citizens of Canada.

Yours very truly,

Thomas Lee York

In response to which I received, less than a month later, the following reply:

March 5, 1963

Dear Mr. York:

Enclosed you will find an SS Form No. 127, Current Information Questionnaire which we are requesting that you complete and return. You should also furnish the board with a copy of your marriage license. You may, if you wish, mail or bring your copy of this instrument to this local board and we will obtain the necessary information therefrom, returning to you immediately.

We also wish to advise that until you become a naturalized citizen of Canada, and have furnished the board with a notarized statement to that effect, you will remain under the jurisdiction of this local board, subject to Selective Service Regulations under the Universal Military Training and Service Act, as amended, and we should be notified at all times of any change of address, occupation or marital status.

You will be classified into Class 1-A not subject to call at the present time, until such time as we hear from you further.

BY DIRECTION OF THE BOARD:

Bernice H. Purvis,
Clerk

Dear Beauteous Board! the jewel of the just, the dragon of the land, the promptest of all my correspondents (more prompt even than my mother to reply): you would not leave me comfortless, you would call to me, within a week you would send me an "Order to Report"!

But by that time I had met and made friends with Peter Taylor, a reporter on the *Citizen* who had grown up in New Brunswick and worked on the railroad there. And because he had never met anyone with such a woodward urge as mine, he had called a friend of his in Moncton, who had called a friend of his in Bathurst, who had said that, sure, if I was fool enough to want to winter there, I could use his cabin at Bartibog Station in the Gaspé, provided I knew how to light a fire and wouldn't burn the bush down. So Peter, after promising to drive you, Lynn, to Moncton, and to put you on the train for Bartibog to join me, and after seeing to it that I was equipped with a parka and snowshoes, put me on a train for New Brunswick.

As the train pulled out of Moncton and passed Newcastle, heading North and gathering steam for the long wilderness grade before stopping briefly to expel me where normally it did not stop, as the cars clickety-clicked over small bridges spanning swamp and between sentrylike columns of spruce, I scribbled on paper provided by the French-Canadian porter (and using a map of Canada that he supplied me) an appendix to the Selective Service current information questionnaire:

March 7, 1963

Mailing Address: For the next 4 or 5 years I will be living a nomadic life along the following route: from within 75 miles of Bathurst, New Brunswick, on a line with Cape Breton Is., northeast across the Gulf of St. Lawrence by coracle and overland through Newfoundland, then north along the Labrador Highlands to Hudson Strait and across to Baffin Is. (which by snowshoe will take about 2 years) to Pond Inlet and across to Devon and Ellesmere Islands, from thence to Lands End and the start of the Polar Cap, where I will either die or return. Should I return I will perhaps at that time apply for Canadian citizenship. Until that time, there are no mail routes handy.

My wife I will deposit at a cabin approximately 75 miles south of Bathurst, my point of departure. More exact location would place it in the midst of the Serpentine Mountains. The Canadian National RR runs within 25 miles of it, and that is its closest line with civilization. So she also will have no address.

The only stable address I can give is that of my parents, Mr. & Mrs. H. C. York, Little Rock, Arkansas.

In the event of a change of plans, or of permanent

settlement, I will certainly contact the board immediately.

These *mirabilia dicta* I stuffed in the envelope (postage paid by the United States Government) and gave to the porter to mail—my parting fillip to civilization and its constraints. Then as the train slowed and lurched to a stop, I opened the door and bailed out into the deep snow and dark night of the frozen spruce bush, Bartibog Station. The train was already pulling out, chugging into the darkness, leaving me standing alone on the track in a vast and silent place, the only sound the receding train, the only sight amid ragged sprucetops silhouetting on every side a sky that stretched off into blackness, the yellow caboose light growing feeble and small until, twinkling like a tiny star, it disappeared into the dark.

THE FIRST WINTER

Four

"Bartibog Sta." read the sign across the squat little telegraph building. Behind it on a wooden platform stood a hand-pump for water, and directly in front and overhanging the track dangled a mailhook. Not a scheduled train stop, not anymore. Not since the two or three families of Swedes who prior to World War I had tried, and failed, to establish a market farm there, had pulled up stakes and left behind them houses, barns, and sheds. Now along the mile or so of track between the spurline to the iron mine and the bridge beyond the station were clustered two deserted farms, the snow-buried shanty that we found out later was lived in, the old deserted house that Father Murdock had moved into; the telegraph station; the sectionmen's brick bunkhouse, and Harold Godin's "camp," in which we lived. Each of these seven buildings fronted on the railroad track; some, like Harold Godin's cabin and Father Murdock's house, were set back fifty yards; but the telegraph station and the section-men's bunkhouse fronted square on the track.

I can scarcely remember my first week there. For some reason, neither the telegraph operator nor the sectionmen were around that week, and I was, so far as I could tell, the only living soul in Bartibog. True, Harold Godin came by train from Bathurst to "show me around," and stomped about the cabin, and from the cabin to the outhouse, and from the outhouse to the woodshed, then back to the cabin with an armload of wood, with which he violently stoked the woodstove, muttering expletives and cursing the whole while, mainly to himself and mostly in French, then deliver-ing with a comprehensive sweep of both hands his summary statement: "If anything gets in th' way, fire it into th' wood-shed!" He proceeded to demonstrate with two or three items —a Catholic doily, a "Home Sweet Home" plaque, some boxes of shotgun shells—"just fire 'em t' hell in th' shed!" Then he crouched on the edge of the kitchen chair and, glancing quickly at his pocket watch, yanked from his hip pocket a half pint of Black Diamond rum. He took a swig and, wiping his mouth with the back of his hand, passed it: "Have a pull a' black death, an' good luck t' you." When I didn't respond right away, "'S watered a bit. What all th' railroaders drink. I'm goin' on sixty-seven, an' never hurt me none. No? Well, I forgot to show you th' cellar—see th' trap-door? He'p yourself t' what's there." Then he was gone, vig-orously snowshoeing back to the track to wave down the four-ten.

The rest of that week I can scarcely recall. I remember the trees, and the high white drifts, and how the snow was always falling everywhere. But you, Lynn, were soon to be-come such a part of everything, that I can hardly be said to have noticed anything—not the deepening snow, nor the brush-and-ink forest, nor the deserted houses and track—un-til the second week, when you arrived.

You came, as I had, on the 4:00 A.M. local, and were dropped with considerably more ceremony into the darkness and snow. This time the train actually came to a full dead stop, and, not only the quizzical French-Canadian porter, but the brakeman as well was there to assist you. The smile on your face, as you stepped off the train, was the bravest thing ever concocted to cover up fear. You came dressed in ski pants and a ski sweater, while loosely draped over your shoulders and hooding your waist-length blond hair was an old Air Force parka with its "Div. Nord" patch and insignia still sewn on. But you came. As I caught you and held you I remember thinking that your hair smelled clean and your shoulders were thin and that I mustn't let you carry too much. Then the train was leaving, the trainmen waving, and we were walking single file down the track with our gear, then scrabbling up the six-foot snowbank that fronted the track with only one snowshoe each (for the whole time we were there, we had only the one pair of snowshoes), and struggling and floundering through the deep drifts with our gear to the door of our cabin.

You slept for two days, while I got up wood; and for a week you refused to visit the outhouse. Part of that time we were stormbound, and the drifts were deep, and to snowshoe across the blizzardy yard, then sit on top of the outhouse while undoing the iced snowshoestraps, then to drop down into the narrow free space around the door where the snow always swirled, and to wrench open the door (which swung outward!) wide enough to squeeze in— all this so as to sit bare-bottomed on an icy board whose hole was surrounded by ridges of snow that had sifted in through the chinks; you refused, nor can I say that I blame you. But it was a problem I couldn't solve for you, and I left you to make your own peace with nature.

After the first couple of days following your arrival, we took stock of ourselves in our new situation, and considered how best to explore our surroundings and do the work required for survival. It wasn't midwinter, really, it was mid-March; but March that had come in like a lion was sunk in a long winter's nap—snow six feet deep, nights fifteen hours long, temperature twenty degrees below zero. Certainly, weather like this was unknown where we had come from, and seemed winter to us. The thought that the snow had melted by now in Ottawa and Toronto, or that jonquils were already in bloom in North Carolina and Arkansas, never occurred to us. Just as well that it didn't; for we tackled the six weeks of winter ahead as one might an Arctic ordeal, and spring, which came late to the Gaspé that year, came none too soon for us.

We still didn't know there was anyone else living near us, and had seen neither human nor animal signs nor movement of any sort, except for the train, which passed nightly and the snow, which never ceased falling. We fancied ourselves as alone as Adam and Eve, and assigned tasks accordingly: yours were to build fire, fetch water, and cook; mine to get wood, find meat, and dispose of the garbage, if any. There was the limiting factor, also, of only one pair of snowshoes. At no time, so long as the snow remained deep, would we be able to traipse far together. It was that simple and seemingly trivial fact that dictated the daily pattern of your being outdoors every morning, and my being out afternoons. We didn't at first tease ourselves with the question of why we were where we were, or doing what we were doing. Certainly in those early days any answer would have been premature. How could we know what it was we searched for until it had been found? Or how could we say what the quest was until it was behind us? Besides, we were too busy doing what needed to be done to question why we did it. Having put ourselves in that situation—and a pleasant situation it was—certain tasks had to be done, and we instinctively did them.

And so, from the time the Moncton–Campbellton express passed at 4:00 A.M. every morning, you would be up and hauling in logs and splitting kindling with which to build a fire; for our cookstove, a magnificent piece as big as a bed that must have cost old man Godin some effort to bring in, had one drawback: the firebox was too small, unless coal was used, to hold embers all night. The sensible thing would have been to let it go out every evening in time to set the next fire; then all you would have needed to do the next morning would be to strike a match. But often I wouldn't get in from my afternoon tramps until long after dark, and then we would stay up reading by lantern, reading and rereading the two books we had brought with us. *Paradise Lost* and the dictionary. So that by 4:00 A.M., when the express passed, cutting sharply and swiftly through the otherwise unbroken silence of the long winter night, you would hop out of bed before the heat from last night's fire had completely seeped from the room, and begin building next morning's fire. (Neither of us was yet acclimatized to the cold.) And since the train was our only reminder of anything other than stillness and snow, and survival and snow, and snow and survival and stillness, and since its 4:00 A.M. passage was the only event in our otherwise unbroken day, your first act, Lynn, after lighting the lamp, was to run to the window and wave. The train, once the engineer spied your light, would respond with a long whistle blast. And later on we found every morning a newspaper tossed in our path.

But that was not yet; that was after your honeymoon phase with the train; for the train was only the first of your many attempts to make contact—with the outside world, with the shell-shocked priest, with the old sectionman whose birthday cake you made, and, as winter relented and spring advanced, with various animals. But the Moncton–Campbellton express was the first, and early in your courtship with the train, one winter's day you shoveled a path all the way from our door to the track, intending, as soon as you heard the train coming, to run to the track with your lantern in hand and wave. Next morning, as you lay awake in the cold cabin, breathing quietly, listening within yourself to the vast silence that always oppressed you, waiting for the first faraway sound, the first faint murmur of movement, and heard in the distance the gathering rush as of an oncoming tide, you jumped out of bed and lit your lamp and ran and opened the door—only to find between you and the track the same white wall and smooth blankness that had yesterday balked you, with a slight undulation like the trough of a wave to indicate where you had shoveled. I peered out from beneath the bed covers and watched you standing wistful and chilled in the doorway, slowly swinging your lantern and waving, while the train whistled past.

Five

You first became aware that we were not the only inhabitants of Bartibog on one of those lonely cold mornings in March after you'd built the fire and watched the 4:00 A.M. train whistle past. Then, again, would come the deep silence; I would still be in bed asleep; and as you stoked the fire and rustled up breakfast and awaited the dawn to fetch water—about seven o'clock, by the first light, you would hear Father Murdock pass. He would be whistling cheerily (we never could distinguish a tune), briskly swinging his bucket, on his way down the track to the pump. The first morning you thought it was birds whistling. Then, the second morning, by the time you strapped on the snowshoes and had tramped out to the track, and along the track to the pump, he was gone—disappeared into one of those seemingly deserted old houses. You looked to see which had smoke, but none appeared to, and you lost his trail on the train tracks.

One cold morning you caught him, and accompanied him to the pump, and you two fetched water together, and walked back along the track to our path where, with a cheery wave and a bob of the head, he bid you good day and went on—the stocky, white-haired, sixty-five-year-old priest of Bartibog, and the pretty, svelte girl with blond hair, both carrying buckets, both smiling and nodding, bidding one another *"Bonjour!"* You were startled by his clerical collar, and could never understand how he kept it so white, or, for that matter, why he wore it. But whenever we saw him his ruddy round face was framed, above, by the black wool toque with wisps of white hair, and below by the black clerical shirt and white collar. And, truly, he was a study in contrasts: cheery and warm and personable, but unable to converse, if it were with the Pope, for more than five minutes at most. It was the sectionmen, his ersatz parishioners, who informed us that he had been shell-shocked, and had lived in the woods since the first war; but whether that was the reason, or that his bishop had sent him to celebrate Mass in the woods, or that God had directed him there to guide us, who knows? We who didn't know why we were in Bartibog might wonder at a priest's presence there. But we were too preoccupied with our own *raison d'être* to searchingly question his. What we did know, because Father Murdock showed us, was that he wrote little fables, in which animals spoke, for a Newcastle Sunday school paper. A pleasant and, whether or not he had been shell-shocked, a harmless enough pastime.

But how disappointed you must have been, Lynn, when after numerous trips to the pump together, and one fine morning a visit to his house, you discovered for yourself that Father Murdock was only good for five minutes' company. The best you could do was to catch him in one of his routines, and these, after a time, you had charted: the 7:00 A.M.

trip to the pump; the 1:00 P.M. trip to the telegraph station
for mail; and, except on bad days when a blizzard was blow-
ing, the early evening walk behind the house. On one occasion, it's true, you talked him into taking a circuitous route
home from the pump, and he showed you the fiddlehead
ferns and morels that were beginning to push through the
snow; but the entire expedition consumed only ten minutes,
he began to get irritable toward the end, and you were left
pondering the first signs of spring while Father Murdock,
quicker than winter, vanished into his house.

Or what about the time you visited him, full of apologies
and armed with a loaf of bread you had baked, at his house?
He received you graciously and seated you, then excused
himself to go upstairs into the cold (as it turned out later, to
shave), while you were left looking about at the room
warmed by a pot-bellied stove and insulated with books—
the walls *were* books, books from the floor to the ceiling,
row upon row of books stacked one on top of the other and
completely lining the large central room in which were a
cot, a table, a chair—the chair you sat in—and the stove; but
except for the books and the fire in the stove, you sat in a
house as dilapidated as the deserted houses. When then he
came down and you gave him the bread, and he gave you
some Sunday school papers, after about five minutes, mostly
spent stoking the fire, he hopped up and hurriedly walked to
the door and ushered you onto the porch—ostensibly to
show you the ermine that lived under his house, but really
to get rid of you.

Father Murdock! Father Murdock! Standing on your
porch that fine spring morning with the blue-eyed, blond-
haired girl, couldn't you hear a hand's-breadth away what I
sensed from the next cabin? Couldn't you leave for a moment the gun-gray forests of Ardenne for the spruce bush of
Bartibog? Couldn't you set aside for a morning your animal

fables for a walk in the woods or a talk in the house with the warm, palpitating, well-educated girl who stood before you on the porch, eager to talk and to be taught?

"Open up!"

"To whom? Who are you?"

"I want to come into your heart to you."

"Then it is a small space you wish."

"What does that matter? Though I scarcely find room, you will have no need to complain of crowding. I will take delight in the things which to you, who have seen them a thousand times, seem routine. The way a rabbit, when startled, backtracks on himself; or how a spruce hen at certain times of the year sits stupidly staring and blinking and can be easily captured. Or how an ermine's fur changes color from season to season, so that there is no such thing as a silver ermine in summer. Or how a moose standing quietly in the dense foliage can be detected. All these and many other little perceptions I would delight in, because I am naturally curious and inquisitive and enthusiastic, and I haven't lived in the woods long enough to be able to see them myself. Won't you show me, or tell me what to look for?"

"I do not wish to appear rude, but this is no place for a woman, it is no place for a man, it is no place at all. I am not here, and you are not here, and we are not here together, for I have my books and my Sunday school papers, and you have . . . what have you? Bonjour, Madame—"

But while you were discouraged in your efforts to befriend Father Murdock, you were undaunted in your exploration of the clearing around Bartibog Station. Every old house and abandoned shed you commandeered for search, unearthing amid old bone-dry timbers held together with wooden pegs such treasures as an ox yoke, a box of rusty steel traps, and a cracked but otherwise functional hurricane lamp. In one deserted barn—built, we found out later, by a

Swede who had come over to homestead, and put up house and barn, and cleared and broken the soil, and planted, then committed suicide—you found nestled in the corner a litter of fox pups. You played with them and put out food for them, but when you returned the next day, they were gone. The whiskey jacks too, and snow buntings, the swallows that nested in the barn that had collapsed, and the rabbit in the woodpile—you tried to coax and tame them all, but all of them shied from you. I told you that if you sat still in the woods, the animals would come to you; but you were too eager to sit still long, and trusted everything living. The moose you tracked and overtook snorting in a snowdrift— when you held out a handful of sugar he reared up flailing with his forelegs and would have trampled you, but you managed to backstep on your snowshoes, and he floundered in the deep drift. You didn't succeed in feeding him, but you got close—close enough to see that, at that distance, a moose's eyes are bloodshot.

Six

Morning by morning the strong March sun was shifting from the south, and rising from a more easterly direction over the frozen spruce bogs. Soon, with the days lengthening, we would be able to see the 4:00 A.M. train without the aid of a lantern, and to explore the half-mile clearing on either side of the track without the bother of snowshoes. Many fine days, Lynn, you spent your mornings poking about the old houses, while I stayed at home and taught myself classical Hebrew from a grammar Father Murdock had lent me. How it came to pass that in Bartibog Station, New Brunswick, snowbound with a young, pretty wife, I devoted my mornings to conning by rote a dead language, was as follows.

On blizzardy days, and most evenings by lamplight, when you were bored with your chores, you would make a game of learning "inkhorn words" from the dictionary, while I read *Paradise Lost*. And reading and rereading *Paradise Lost*, I got sidetracked again and again by Milton's numerous references to Old Testament names. Their very sounds intrigued me: Chemosh, Dagon, Ashtaroth. I thought that I had missed something as rich as nature itself in not having read the Bible, and gradually I determined to do so. But in order to read it thoroughly, and experience it deeply, I should try to believe as I read; for, as with the bush, so with the book: only by plunging myself to its heart would I feel I had truly tried it. For me this meant learning, first, Hebrew, then Greek, which morning by morning I set myself to.

And, now that I think on it, it was I, your husband, and not Father Murdock, a stranger, who refused to let you come into his heart and who wanted to be left alone. I wanted you off in the mornings while I studied in the one-room cabin, then I would be off all afternoon and until long after dark—a pattern that the one pair of snowshoes enforced. So life at Bartibog Station that winter must have been lonely for you until, around Easter, the strong young sun started loosening the land and rotting the high snowdrifts.

There were, now that the weather was starting to break, and frost beginning to work on railroad steel, five or six sectionmen to be seen around Bartibog Station. For about three nights of every week they came on their track motorcar from wherever they'd worked that day to overnight at their bunkhouse. We could hear their car throbbing in the deep silence of the frozen bog—a pulsating *thump! thump!* that I often confused with the beat of the wings of an oversexed spruce cock. Whenever I heard the *thump! thump!* beginning, the two-cylinder motor warming up slowly and mounting to a crescendo, I would run to the track and gaze vainly in either direction, then shake my head in wonderment that two things so unlike—a track motorcar and a spruce cock—

could sound so similar. In some such manner must nature adapt to the encroachment of man, the difference being that the sectionmen's car patrolled the track the year round, while the spruce cock strove to allure a hen only in springtime and fall.

One of the sectionmen, Elmer—I have forgotten his surname, but let the name "Elmer of Bartibog" be emblematic of the man—was forever watching our cabin and, whenever I was out for the day, and the sectionmen in, dropping by to visit you. He would knock at the door and, when you let him in, sit down and follow your movements with his narrow fox-face, insinuating in his Elmerish way that his visits could have a point. At first you welcomed any company, even Elmer's, but when his repertoire of small talk in a *patois* of English and French had been spent—which it had with his thumbnail sketch of each sectionman there, and of how beastly lonely all of them were—when then he lapsed into his leering silence, riveting on you his narrow eyes as you moved about the cabin cooking and sweeping; then your mind began devising ways to get rid of him, or reasons to go out yourself. Only once did you visit the sectionmen's bunkhouse, and that was a time when you spied Elmer coming, and slipped out and around the back way.

The bunkhouse was a relatively modern brick building, built during the fifties and equipped (for what more strategic target than Bartibog Station?) with a bomb shelter, which the sectionmen used as a huge underground garbage bin. The men, on that one occasion when you visited them, scurried about the dim lantern-lit room colliding and trying to keep from cursing while picking up clothes and adjusting suspenders, in an attempt to make themselves and their bunkhouse more presentable. They were as astonished as you were: they at your arrival, long after dark, at their door; you at the stench and smokiness, the dirty socks dangling from clotheslines that crossed and crisscrossed the room, the closeness and messiness of their bunkbeds, and the food scraps and spent cans and week's dirty dishes which filled the sink and cluttered the table and overflowed onto the floor of the kitchen.

This for your first impression, the utter dinginess of the place; and for your second, their extreme, almost exaggerated, politeness. They invited you in, and you went in; they had been playing cards, but they stopped. They seated you in their only good chair, which they made sure was clean before you sat down; then, while old Baptiste excused himself to make tea, which you politely declined, the rest sat around on straight-backed chairs and answered as well as they could in broken English the questions you put to them.

What was the strange noise we heard at nighttime? The weird bellowing: Was it wolves? Was it moose?

All laughed, and pointed to old Baptiste: he stepped outside each night before going to bed to howl like a wolf and bellow like a moose; he was an old man now, without family.

How old was he?

Too old. His birthday would be next week.

What about their families? And why weren't their wives here with them?

They didn't understand the question, and, when they did, were astonished and laughed heartily. Pictures came out: of their wives, their children; many children, work-worn wives in faded black-and-white photos, standing before small, clapboard, lookalike houses—in Campbellton, Dalhousie, Bathurst, Newcastle. All, except Elmer, took the train home each weekend to visit their families.

Then Baptiste, after you had accepted and sipped some tea and were making ready to go, took you aside to ask if Elmer was bothering you. They had discussed it, he said, and they had warned Elmer; tomorrow the whole group was going to see Father Murdock—that would fix Elmer.

At about that time Elmer came in, looking, as soon as he saw you there and felt the others' cold, steely stares, like a fox caught in a trap. His loud brassy greeting froze midsyllable, and he slunk aside as Baptiste, ignoring him, ushered you out to walk you home.

The next morning—a fine, clear, cold day, a working day, if ever there was one—we watched the sectionmen go, a solid delegation, up the track, and turn in at Father Murdock's. Often they would go to his place in the early evening, singly or in pairs, and "make wood" for him. We would hear the dull thuds of axes and see them splitting the cedar and spruce they had piled near his house into stove lengths and kindling. But never, since they were away on the weekends, had we seen the whole group (except Elmer) go to Father Murdock's and boldly knock on his door and actually enter his house! They were inside a long time, as visits with Father Murdock are measured, approximately twenty minutes. Then they came out and boarded their track motorcar, once again without Elmer, and we could hear its throbs, like those of a spruce cock, fading down the track into stillness.

A little later Father Murdock emerged from his house. He was bare-headed, as he often was on fine days, and had on his clerical shirt and white collar as usual. But what we had not seen before, and what he wore on this occasion instead of his sweater or parka, was a black cassock, which reached full to the ground. As he passed white-haired and without whistling between the high banks of snow, he had the look of a punishing angel whose hair has turned hoar in the knowledge that no one, neither man nor beast, could withstand the face of his cold.

A week later, at old Baptiste's birthday party, at which the whole gang was present, when you wrapped a piece of the cake in a napkin to be taken to Father Murdock, the sectionmen yelled, "Elmer will take it!" Elmer sat glaring while the others all laughed, his eyes narrowed nearly to slits. Then he jumped up, snatched up the napkin, stalked to the door, and whirled around.

"Two things I don't like about that old priest," he growled.

"What's that, Elmer?" Some of the men could scarcely speak for laughing and pointing at him.

"His face!" he snarled, and slammed out, carrying the cake by its napkin like a hurt hand in a sling.

Seven

Beside the woodpile he burrows, beneath the snowdrift, the old trapper of Bartibog. The trapper sits in his six-foot-high shanty, its stovepipe periscoping the snow from which one day you spied smoke ascending; he squats amid filth on the dirt floor strewn with offal and animal waste—two muskrat, a wolverine pelt, a lynx hide and head partially severed from the pink carcass, a bucket of blood, and fat scrapings. The walls of his hovel are overlapped ovals of drying beaver skins, the roof is of tin, the door is of poles, and there are no windows. He squats on the floor before the gas drum that serves as a stove, on whose rickety top split beaver tails are being rendered to lard. And as he squats, hunched forward and hairy before the oily, flickering flame, he curses and scrapes a wolverine skin, scrapes and curses.

From his hole in the snow the old trapper was just emerging the day we went to visit him—on his way to the pump,

toting three empty buckets; when one fell he gave it a savage kick and strode on, while we ran alongside. He scarcely
noticed us, though he muttered at us the whole way, and I
think that inauspicious beginning was one of the reasons
you never warmed to him, Lynn. There were others: his
bent six-foot frame and his swarthy hooked face combined
to give him a vulpine look. And he was coarse—foul-
mouthed and evil-looking and ill-smelling. But what you
mainly disliked about him, I think, was that I was so taken
with him, in spite of his cursing in French. His muttered re-
frain that first morning, interspersed with incidental curses
at the snow, the railroad track, and the pump, was directed
against a wolverine which had got free of a trap. The wolverine had carefully chewed its leg off, thus spoiling the fur;
but the trapper had managed to catch the brute by tracking
its blood in the snow, and was now skinning its pelt out. As
we neared the door of his hovel, he gathered up twenty
miles' worth of curses into a peroration:

"*Loup la biche!* Dirtiest *biche* in the woods! Pelt's spoilt,
an' th' brute snapped at me! They're so dirty," and now the
old trapper, in a paroxysm of rage, looked me straight in the
eye, "they'll chew theirselves in half, just for spite. *Loup la
biche!*"

This fulmination delivered, he stopped to enter the hovel,
sloshing some water on the ground as he did so and cursing
vehemently. He beckoned impatiently and we followed him
in, but you were reluctant. Nor can I say that I blame you:
the stew of carcasses inside, by the flickering light from the
stove, was ghastly enough, even obscene; but with three
persons crowded into the windowless room, the stench near
the ceiling where all the heat went was nearly unbearable.
You stood near the door with your arm to your face, breathing into your parka, only your eyes visible, while I stooped
down beside the trapper who showed me, off-handedly and
surprised that I should be interested, the various skins lying

about. He ended with the wolverine pelt which, as he took it up to work on again, he spat at viciously. "Dirty *biche!*" he snarled.

You stood watching, waiting impatiently, and trying not to breathe at all, thinking: "What could be dirtier than an old trapper?"

But even you would have to admit that, eventually, our acquaintance with the old French-Canadian proved helpful; for we who in six weeks' time had consumed the stock of canned goods in Harold Godin's root cellar were reduced to a small sack of flour, from which you made bannock, and about five pounds of brown rice. The day after we met him, the old trapper took me with him to run his nearest trapline, and I came back from the snowshoe marathon (the whole trip was about twenty-six miles) gall-footed and weary, but with a forty-pound beaver carcass—"pork of the woods," he called it—which lasted us a full week. Thereafter, the trapper, whenever he slept at his hovel, which he did about every two weeks, would bring us a beaver, or a muskrat, or moose meat; and once, when he was too burdened with furs to haul meat, he deposited outside our door (where he left meat whenever he brought it; he would never come in) two steel traps and a jarful of beaver testes for bait. Shriveled and vile-smelling they were, just the thing to allure beaver. But the only beaver I ever killed was one I met on the path (he was changing streams, and was as surprised as I was), and, at the insistence of the old trapper who was beside me, I ran after the beaver, and because he was so fat, caught up with him and banged him on the head with my ax. That beaver died on dry land, and the trapper, having observed my performance, counseled me not to pursue hunting as a vocation. (He had already warned me against trapping.) By such advisements, and from watching the trapper run his traplines—plunging his hands in the icy cold water, wading in after drowned beaver and muskrat, and bludgeoning otter to death—I knew that I wasn't destined to the profession. But should I decide to try trapping, he always added after advising me not to, he would sell me his traps and drying frames, and throw in his shanty too, for twenty-five dollars.

The amazing thing, as I look back on it now, is that throughout the entire time we were in Bartibog we were never asked why we were there. The priest, the trapper, and the sectionmen all knew why they were there, but they spared us the embarrassment of having to give an account of ourselves. And well that they did; for certainly the nature of the search is that no one knows what he searches for until he has found it. And therefore it is rude to interrogate others. Where do you come from? What are you here for? Who are you, really? Such questions are affronts and insults. That, at least, is the ancient wisdom of many primitive cultures, and is it not also the gist of the Christian ethic? Better to befriend than to offend, since the befriended or offended party may turn out to be a messenger from the Almighty. For the seeker looks for hints and hieroglyphs in every face and every track he meets, and this demands a high degree of concentration, which in turn requires restraint of the senses. And both restraint of the senses and concentration of the mind are difficult if not impossible to achieve in a social setting, where an excess of energy is squandered in relationships, and where the natural rhythms of the body and the mind are idly heightened by casual contact with others. Thus the need, in any serious attempt to know oneself, for withdrawal; for the mind, left alone and allowed to respond, will exfoliate like a flower; but forced to answer inquisitive questions, or to perform repetitive stunts, as the wheel follows the foot of the ox that draws the wagon, the mind atrophies.

When I came into the North Woods, and snowshoeing among silent trees had all my time in my own hands, I resolved to spend it all, whatever it cost me, in search of—I knew not what, but something I had not yet found, without which life was not worth the living. In which I was so determined that I chose rather to leave my country, flaunt my father, and submit you, Lynn, to the rigors of woods life, than to allow my mind, in a preordained rut devoted to higher education, national defense, harvest, and hog slaughter, to atrophy. And God, whether He put that desire in my mind, or whether He is mind itself, saw fit to fulfill in us and for us (not only for us, though; for there have been many who, each with his own woodward urge, have experienced a similar fulfillment) the promise proclaimed by the prophet:

> I will make with them a covenant of peace and banish wild beasts from the land, so that they may dwell securely in the wilderness and sleep in the woods.
> And I will make them and the places round about my hill a blessing; and I will send down the showers in their season; they shall be showers of blessing.

But it was long before we experienced the peace and secureness spoken of by the prophet, or ever dreamed of relating our winter in Bartibog to a scriptural promise having to do with "covenant of peace" and "showers of blessing." Covenants and blessings were to us meaningless, and to describe our meager subsistence in such terms would have seemed ludicrous. For as the sun must first thaw the snows of winter, while stirring the roots of the crocus, before the crocus can thrust through the crust of spring and open its head to the air, so the gentle influence of nature will open the brutalized mind, but first the mind must be emptied, the roots of intelligence stirred, and artificial and learned responses unlearned.

This purging the mind of false images and stale thoughts, the first step of the quest and the only one over which we have any control, was, without my realizing it, what my afternoon and evening walks were all about. And it was these walks that had predisposed me to be fascinated with the old trapper. For after reading in Hebrew every morning a chapter or two from the prophets, I would be gone afternoons and until after dark—ostensibly I was out "hunting." But I never came home with anything other than the single-shot .22 rifle, or the ax that I carried, and tales of the wildcat I tracked. This wildcat became my obsession. I would discover his tracks in the most forlorn places and follow as they led me full circle, or until they disappeared over ice. Often I found, still steaming with warmth, the lynx's lean pencil-stools, which to me in my single-minded pursuit seemed like God's scoriae. I imagined encounters and ambushes, and checked every tree, especially when walking the hardwood ridges by which the barren bog sloped toward the distant Serpentine Mountains. On more than one occasion I found myself, with night falling, and I having futilely spent the entire afternoon following the tracks of the foraging wild-cat, lost in a maze of animal tracks in the midst of the frozen spruce bog. Then I would stop and look for the North Star, and, if the sky was dark, listen; and once out of the great empty silence that seemed to diminish and aggrandize me both, but most to desolate me, came the sound of a distant train whistle. I began trudging in the direction I thought it came from and then, when I heard it again, it seemed to come from the opposite side; and so on again, until the train, still as distant as ever, seemed to taunt and encircle me, and I was as lost as before. Somehow I got home, long, long after dark, and found you waiting for me.

I might have spent all those days and nights inside with you instead of out tracking the wildcat, for the wildcat I never encountered until, later, reading one of Lancelot Andrewes' sermons—again, borrowed from Father Murdock —I came to the line, "Christ is no wildcat. . . ." But by then

I was over my wildcat obsession, because, priest and trapper and sectionmen notwithstanding, we had run out of food and winter at the same time, and moved deeper into the woods, to Mile 9.

Eight

It grieves me that so many share the name of woman. It ought to be a richly deserved title, crowning a lifetime of achievement. When I consider, Lynn, how you packed into two winters and a summer a lifetime's worth of trial and hardship, enduring poverty for love's sake, it shames me that so many who will not suffer inconvenience bear the same name—woman. I fancy there are few alive who, while still young, would renounce their comforts to follow, always cheerful, where love led. I know of none. Man or woman, discontent with what they have but unwilling to renounce it, all shirk hardship.

But hardship in itself is no virtue; nor is deprivation, unless it be embraced and entered into as a means to something more. We moved to Mile 9 on the spurline to the iron mine because spring was coming, the woods and waterways were opening, and there would be more fish and game there. So we were seeking, if not comfort, greater self-sufficiency in our hunting, fishing, and food-gathering attempts. Fish and game we found, and ferns and greens and leeks, but the shack we lived in at Mile 9 was the most uncomfortable place we ever lived in. For bed, ropes stretched across two wooden frames stuffed with spruce boughs. For table, a rough-hewn bench; for bench, the floor. A door of poles on leather hinges and without a screen; a square of window which did not open; an old oildrum with two holes, for fuel and flue, made do as heater. An orange crate nailed above the window served for shelves; another crate beside the bunk was our footlocker. The cabin's slanted roof was made of poles with gravel packed on top and moss between; its walls were railroad ties which, when the door was closed and the stove was on, reeked of creosote. Were what went on within those walls the story of Mile 9, that spring of 1963, would have been dull indeed; for we were constantly colliding with each other in the dim light of the heater and struggling to keep ourselves in food.

The cabin, which had been built by the sectionmen as a hunting camp, sat flush on the spurline about midway between Bartibog and the iron mine, and as spring advanced, the melting snow revealed a pile of scrap lumber, which you, Lynn, stacked and restacked in an effort at neatness, and from which we foraged all our stove wood. The camp at Mile 9 was much rougher than the cabin at Bartibog, but it sat in woods vibrant with wildlife, and near a river teeming with fish.

The first fine day of spring (it must have been May Day, for it was the day the mayflies came out) we were up with the sun to go fishing. All along the spurline snowdrifts were melting, and the ice in the river had thawed, but patches of ice still sparkled on ponds, and frost crystallized the mud, making walking difficult. With each step my boots would crunch through the layer of frost and squish in the mud, while you, who were lighter, sometimes got through, sometimes not. By the time we reached the pond, about a quarter mile from the cabin, we were in mud to the knees, and our faces and hands were smeared with mire. But we cut alder poles and tied on hooks and lines and looked around us for bait.

As I say, it must have been May Day. For as the sun warmed the shallow pond's surface, thousands of tiny gray cocoons, indistinguishable in color and size from the twigs and leaves that littered the pond, began to quiver and move on the face of the water, wimpling its glassy surface as when water bugs skitter at evening. Then, at the same time as the mayflies came fluttering upward—clumsily and heavily rising from the pond's surface to a few feet above it, fluttering downward again, floating helplessly in the water, struggling to ascend again—at the same May Day moment, warmed by the same solar heat, and wakened from the same winter torpor, rainbow trout by the hundreds, the spawn of previous springs, began to surface all over the pond: leaping high in the air after the fluttering mayflies, gulping, falling, then leaping again. The entire surface of the wilderness pond was suddenly roused into springtime; even the frogs, along the dead branches of sunken trees, hopping crazily after the mayflies.

We stood on the bank dumfounded at the display. Then, at the sight of a drunken lunge by what must have been the granddaddy trout of the pond, a four- or five-pounder, I grabbed my alder pole, hook, and line, and waded wildly into the pond, snatching as I went a handful of mayflies out of the air and stuffing them on the hook. Standing waist deep in water, surrounded by surfacing fish (and looking foolish, I know, for you stood on the bank laughing till tears came to your eyes), I wielded my blunt alder pole like a fly rod, flipping the hook with its mass of mayflies here, there, and every time it struck the water, a big trout took it, until after a time when the trout ceased to lunge and simply rolled and lolled on the surface, gorging themselves, and my hookful of flies ceased to catch them, we found that, May Day or any day, the dorsal fin cut from a caught trout would catch another.

As I excitedly caught fish after fish, and tossed them to you on the bank, pole and all, for you to take off the hook—which at first you were squeamish to do—and showed you how to tap them over the head so they wouldn't flop on the ground, how I wished my father were there. A single day's fishing like that, I felt sure, would persuade him of the rightness of our having come North. Wasn't a day like that worth a decade of troubles? Wasn't a May Day worth the whole winter? We took that day from the little two-acre pond more trout than we could eat, though we gorged ourselves as the trout had; and the one I caught last, about a four-pounder, had a belly as big as his body—a full pound at least of gulped and still quivering mayflies. Never again would he, or, for that matter, we, experience such a May Day: for he was nearly insensible when we caught him, and we, after feeding on him and his fellows, lay insensible two days in our cabin.

But May Day isn't every day, and I soon tired of fishing and grew moody again, while our regular food provisioning fell to you. Initially you had been squeamish, but now every fine morning you went with your alder pole and hook and line to fish, not only in the bog ponds along the spurline, but also in the river behind the cabin. Like Neolithic woman, who fished and gardened while her useless husband dabbled in magic or hunted aimlessly, you picked fiddlehead ferns and dug leeks and plucked mushrooms, and every morning caught enough trout for our supper. There was in the river behind our cabin, below an otter slide, a deep sun-dappled pool formed by a giant hemlock, which an enterprising beaver had felled. Here, every afternoon after fishing, you would take off your clothes, let your hair down, and bathe, washing your body all over with the bar of soap you had salvaged from Bartibog, and combing out your long hair, which now fell to below your waist.

One afternoon I came upon you bathing and watched you plunge shivering into the icy pool, breast-stroke across to the log, then clamber up to comb out your hair in a clerestory of sunlight; while an otter on the opposite bank, as though in mimicry of your antics, alternately slid into the water and sunned his sleek fur on the log. You seemed to belong as much as he to the river, and to disturb it as little, as though your long blond hair and his rich black pelt were both, like the bark on the log and the scales of the fish, expressions of the same nature, the same interpenetrating intelligence that quickened in a season such varied colors, textures, and shapes so as to see, smell, feel, and enjoy itself. Why else such variety and richness in nature which, were they not all expressions of the same nature, would be mere oddity and waste? All very well, and many have argued the same, and convincingly, so as to include even the wildcat which Christ is not; but it is difficult to account for the mosquitoes.

The mosquitoes arrived as they attacked, suddenly. Hatching out the first hot day, they arrived that evening; and giving no advance warning, no declaration of war, attacked immediately: whining wave after wave of bloodthirsty bugs buzzing and dive-bombing all our undefended parts, breaking through our meager defenses. We had no screen door, no bed net; and because it was a warm day, we had left even our wood door wide open. Pinned down like refugees by strafing Messerschmitts we lay, throughout that first summer night, the discomfited, outmaneuvered, overwhelmed victims of *Blitzkrieg* . . . ruefully reminding ourselves as we lay on our beds through the long, hot, humid night, smothering ourselves under blankets or slapping our own faces, that we lived in a swamp, in the midst of a bog, the very name of which might have warned us . . . that we were woefully unprepared for such warfare . . . that life in the bush (behind the whine of mosquitoes, and just out of range we could hear the bullfrogs *ba-rooming*) was indeed warfare, and mindless. . . .

Sleepless we lay through the tortuous night, slapping mosquitoes and burying our heads beneath blankets, counting aloud the number we killed (over two hundred), and recalling in gloom (for we had no lantern, not even a candle) details that now seemed as critical as they had seemed trifling before: the jar of Vaseline mixed with citronella, which Baptiste had sent and said we should mix with pine tar; the wrecked and rusty screen door we had spotted at a deserted lumber camp up the track.

These and a spate of other fantastic defenses we conjured up in our pain, and I think it was then, Lynn, that you (like Scarlett O'Hara, who swore she would "rob, cheat, steal if I have to, but I'll never go hungry again!") decided to leave the swamp we were in and devised your trip out. Marvelous how a night of terror will completely change the mind and act as a tonic to the senses. . . . Grimly we lay until finally the sheer frustration of slapping ourselves and the sweaty discomfort of feeling smothered underneath hot, heavy blankets exhausted us, and we slept . . . sunk into brief, troubled sleep. . . . But to this day I believe that, had we not had each other to talk to that night, to be angry at and patient with—to summon from and share with one another the strength of two—either of us singly would have panicked. Strange that so tiny a thing as a mosquito, or even ten thousand mosquitoes, could panic a person . . . unless mosquitoes are, as the Eskimos say, the Devil shattered in pieces. . . .

It was near noon the next day before we emerged, haggard and tired, from beneath blankets, our noses bulbous and faces stippled and eyes swollen shut with bug bites, into the stifling heat and creosote smell of the sun-baked camp at Mile 9. We pried open our eyes, and looked at each other, and laughed (as well as we could through split lips, with swollen tongues, in dry mouths), then staggered from bed and dismantled the oildrum heater and moved it outside. After washing off in the river (and marveling that a thousand mosquito bites, give or take fifty or so, could so change a person's appearance), we cut a gash in a big pine tree and drew some resin to mix in our bug dope. Having cooked the pitch and mixed it well with Vaseline and citronella, we smeared ourselves with the viscous stuff, which resembled, in smell and color and texture, roofing tar. Then we trudged up the track to the deserted pulp mill where, in addition to a wrecked and rusty screen door, we gleaned a kerosene lantern without a mantle, an iron pot without a bail, and a torn and partially rotted tarpaulin. (This last item, though I didn't suspect it then, you wanted for your trip out.) We cooked outside that evening, and worked on the screen door, the lantern, and the chinks in the walls all at once; by nightfall we had secured ourselves and our cabin against another invasion.

Nine

If anyone praises women better than I, I surely will not complain. I would be glad to hear women praised far and wide, though there is only one I will boast of. This does not mean that I disparage all others. A man's boast rings hollow when he applauds his own wife at the expense of his neighbor's. The man's victory is like that of the chess player who, when he had knocked his opponent's queen off the board, crows, "That checkmates them! My queen is the best!" His own queen may be the next to fall, for many a wife has turned traitress. For myself, having found it necessary to trust only one woman, I have found only one woman trustworthy. Still, I am convinced that of all the variable things in this life, a woman's heart is one of the least variable. A woman will undergo hardship and shame and all manner of external trials, and never think any more of them than of the passing seasons, so long as her heart is in trust. But break that trust, and unleash her affections, and you have the ficklest flirt in creation—the tail that wags the dog. So I would never, just because I have been lucky, consider it better to trust women than God. But it is a great mistake, and causes much ill, not to trust women at all.

So tell us now, Lynn, as you told me then, about your marathon trip out and back—of the people you met, the difficulties you had, and how you managed on less than twenty dollars and within four days to retrieve the truck from my grandmother's house at Kennebunk, Maine, where Peter Taylor had left it, and get back to Mile 9 in New Brunswick. The last I remember was seeing you off up the track: clean, but smudge-faced and schoolgirlish looking; for you'd scrubbed in the river but the pine tar wouldn't come off, and you'd dressed in the clothes the Harold Godins had sent you —the French chemise, the long, fancy dress with puffed sleeves (a feedsack cotton print), the little girls' dress shoes (flats, with buckles and straps), and the thin white socks— the sort of outfit Rachel, our five-year-old, might wear to school. But overflowing your pale print dress, and in contrast to your smudged face, your shining blond hair caught the morning sun and adorned you down to the waist. You looked a goddess in disguise, in flimsy feedsack trappings, ready to burst forth full on the world except that the world wasn't ready. Smudge-faced and yellow-haired you traipsed up the track, pausing at the bend before the bridge to wave, and then you were gone . . . walking out of our wilderness winter into the world's summertime. . . .

For the remainder of that day, and the next, and the next, I slouched about camp, doing alone what we'd done together—fishing, cooking, eating, sleeping—but doing them with less gusto, less grace; uneventfully the days passed. I watched the tracks for sight of you, and listened each night for your sound. I remember only the waiting; sleep seemed to have gone from the woods.

And then, as if out of nowhere, you were back, as though

you'd stepped outside the cabin a minute, and a minute later returned: your hair wild and shining, your face radiant, your funny little dress clean. You shot through the door like the sun to the swamp, so quickly that you startled me; and before I could stand or say anything, you were talking excitedly:

"A bear! I met the cutest bear, not fifteen minutes ago, no farther away than that!" With a sweep of your arm indicating the distance between you and me, and then with both arms: "He was *this* big, and I was so scared I sang 'The Teddy-bear Picnic.' He liked it! Every time I started singing a verse, he'd stop and watch me and listen, and whenever I'd stop, he'd start toward me. I sang and sang and sang, the same verse over and over:

> If you go out in the woods today
>   you'd better not go alone,
> You'd better not go to the woods today,
>   you're better to stay at home;
> For all the bears that ever there was
> Will be there just becuz becuz
> Today's the day the teddy bears have their pic-nic!"

Later that evening, after you'd eaten and rested and got over your scare, we lay down together in the dark of the cabin on our bed of spruce boughs, while mosquitoes buzzed vainly at the screen door and the bullfrogs *baroomed* beyond, and you talked low to me until late in the night of your trip out and back and the plans you had made. . . .

"It was a beautiful day, you remember—too hot for bugs— and me sashaying up the track in my funny little dress, the one the Godins had sent me. When I got to the mines—"

"How far is the mines? Is it really nine miles?"

"All of that. Don't interrupt, I'll forget where I was."

"At the mines."

"I didn't go in. I heard it a long way off, then when I saw it—a lot of tin buildings and smokestacks and trucks, and men in hard hats and overalls churning around in the mud— as soon as I saw it off to the right, I left the track and struck off through the woods. I figured there'd be a road some- where near, and there was. But before I got to it, I met them. They—"

"They?"

"Some fishermen—businessmen really, on a fishing trip. They were waiting to be picked up by their guide."

"In the woods?"

"Near a little stream. If you won't interrupt, I'll do better. Poor darling, I know you're eager to hear, and I want to tell you, but I'm awfully tired."

"I promise I won't interrupt."

"Well, I came splashing across this little stream, I was whistling, I think, and I startled the four men who were sit- ting there eating. They hadn't seen me, but I'd spotted them —that was why I was whistling, so as not to surprise them."

"But they were surprised."

"All of them jumped up, and I asked them where was the road to Moncton, and they said their guide had gone for the truck, and I said I didn't have a ride, and they said I could ride with them—they were from Moncton, two of them were, and the other two from Newcastle. So we sat down to wait, and they offered me food, and I saw that they had a few fish.

"'How's the fishing been?' I asked them.

"'No good,' said the one, an insurance man, I think, from Moncton, 'no good at all. They're just not biting, and them that do bite are tiny.' And he showed me their creel; it had six or eight fingerlings in it.

"'Is that the rig you've been using?' I shouldn't have said that, I know. They had fly rods and tackle boxes full of dry flies and wet flies and all sorts of stuff—all that stuff you said your father used to fish with. 'Here,' I said, and whipped out the pocket knife you said I should carry, and walked down to the stream and waded in and cut them an alder pole. Then I rigged a hook and line to it, and since the fish they had were so little, cut off half a tail instead of a fin, and tossed it out. Two or three tosses and I had one—not big, but bigger than any they had. Well, they were dumfounded. All of them went down the bank and hacked at the alders, and by time the guide arrived back with the truck they had two or three big trout each, and I figured I'd better take a back seat. After all, he was the driver, and it was the ride I was after.

"So now we're on the road to Newcastle, and I'm comfortably settled in the back seat, quietly minding my tongue, and the men are feeling pretty good now, and one of them mentions Tulane—"

"Tulane? In New Orleans?"

"That's right. I said before that they were businessmen. And one of them, the banker from Moncton, had a nephew attending Tulane. And before they got dropped off, he was trying to promote their next trip—to New Orleans, for Mardi Gras. Anyway, I couldn't resist.

"'New Orleans makes a good trip,' I said, 'but not at Mardi Gras time.' They all turned and stared at this wild-looking girl from out of the woods who knew all the best fishing methods. 'Oh, I went to Newcomb,' I said, 'graduated from Tulane, just two years ago.' But it was the guide who was most uneasy. He was the grimmest, grimiest New Brunswicker that ever led tourists astray. He just glared at me through the rear-view mirror. I knew I had made a mistake.

"And I had. When we got to Moncton I called the bus depot and found I had just enough money to get from Saint John to Kennebunk, and that the bus had just left. The guide, who by this time had dropped off the others, said he had to go on to Saint John and that I could stay over at his house, with his family. Since I didn't see that I had much choice, I rode on with him, but as it turned out—"

"Why didn't you call Peter Taylor's friends and stay over with them? You were in Moncton."

"I knew you'd get angry. Because I had enough money to get to your grandmother's house from Saint John, and if I went straight on I could catch the next bus, the one that had just left Moncton. I didn't want to stay over if I didn't have to, I was just getting started. You know how it is on a trip."

"So what happened? I hope it wasn't too bad, but whatever it was, tell me now."

"Don't get angry."

"I won't."

"Well, as you might have guessed, this guide, it turned out, had no family, and when he pulled off the road about thirty miles short of Saint John, I started climbing out the passenger side and thanking him profusely."

"Didn't he try to stop you?"

"He tried. But it's pretty hard to stop someone who's determined not to be stopped, unless you resort to force."

"Which he didn't?"

"He thought about it. I told him I was sixteen. In the end, I hitchhiked on into Saint John—nothing to report, a nice old farmer picked me up—and when I arrived, around nine at night, I found I had just missed the bus.

"So here I was in Saint John, New Brunswick, on a Friday night. I figured I could afford to spend thirty cents and still board the 6:00 A.M. bus."

"What in the world did you do?"

"Walked around until I got tired, then found an all-night cafe. It was your typical waterfront all-night cafe, the kind you see in old movies, only I'd never been in one before, except with my father in Mobile, Alabama. When you went in everyone looked you over, and when you sat down they all looked away. It was crowded—a lot of sailors. I sat down at a table by myself, and for an hour I sipped one cup of coffee. Oh, I forgot to mention . . . there was a policeman by the door—a big Irishman with ruddy cheeks and pot belly. After about an hour one of the frowsy-looking women who'd been sitting and laughing at a table with sailors sauntered over to the policeman and said something to him. I could tell it was about me by the way she avoided looking my way. Then the policeman strode over to my table and said in a gruff voice, 'Come with me, please.' That's all he said, but my heart sank. 'I'm just going to order some more coffee,' I said. 'No, you come on with me.' And there was, now that he said it again, a kind of gruff kindness in the way he said it, as though he was trying to convey a kind tone to me while appearing gruff to the others."

"What did you do?"

"I went. Everyone was watching, of course, as I got up to go, but once we were outside he wasn't gruff anymore, he was just kind. He said, 'Are ya new t' Sainjawn?' or something like that, and I said, 'I beg your pardon?' 'A visiter, like?' 'Oh, yes, officer, I'm on my way to Maine—to my grandmother's. My bus leaves at six in the morning.' 'Ya look tired, ya do.' 'I'm dead,' I said, and that was the truth.

"We were walking along the street now, overlooking the harbor, and every time we passed some landmark or other, he would point to it. 'Nice town we got here,' he'd say; or 'That there's a statue of the poor mariners lost at sea, put up by their widows and orphans.'" And then, as though he were pointing out another landmark, 'We've got a fine hotel here, a grand hotel, I want ya to see.'

"It *was* grand—plush carpets, marble foyer, and a gilded, winding staircase. We entered the lobby and he said, adopting again his gruff manner, 'There used to be . . . I'll just check . . . wait here.' He strode over to the desk, and chatted with the desk clerk. The desk clerk glanced over at me and nodded two or three times. Then the policeman strode back. 'Still is,' he said, 'for out-o'-town people, hasn't stayed in this hotel before, trial rooms—I'd like ya t' try one an' then you tell me if this is, or it ain't, a grand hotel. Up this staircase with ya, and turn t' th' left—' All this time he was ushering me across the plush carpet, past the desk, to the foot of the staircase. 'Here's th' key, and somebody'll wake ya in th' mornin' in time for your bus—'

"And then he was gone. And I walked up that gilded, winding staircase, and turned to the left, and opened the door into the finest, cleanest, great good place I have ever seen—for once inside I saw a canopied queen-sized bed with clean, white, freshly ironed sheets, and that looked inviting to me; but even more inviting was the shiny tiled bathroom and shower. Scoff if you like, but the first thing I did was wriggle free of my funny little dress and chemise and turn on the wonderful, welcome hot water. Then I washed the pine tar from my face and skin and forever out of my hair. Then I washed my funny dress and chemise and socks, and hung them up to dry. And when I was washed and warm and thoroughly relaxed, I turned back the sheets on that canopied bed, and I remember thinking as I fell asleep that my mother always kept clean, white, freshly ironed sheets on the beds at home.

"I fell asleep in no time, and it seemed no time before there was a knocking at my door, the sun just coming up over the harbor town and in through my window, and I dressing quick as a rabbit and running to the bus depot, just in time.

"There's really not much more to tell. Your grandmother and aunts thought I looked starved—'the hungry one,' they called me."

"Are they still schoolteachers? Still spinsters? I haven't seen them for years."

"Who would marry your maiden aunts, weighing in at over three hundred pounds each? Your grandmother's shorter, but stout. She called Edna at school and asked her to bring home some food. Flossie ate one entire barbequed chicken before dinner—I'm not exaggerating—and four more at dinner."

"With potatoes enough, I suppose, to feed an army."

"That's right. And peas, and carrots, and artichokes—it fairly stifled my appetite just to see all that food."

"I wouldn't mind seeing it."

"Well, they wouldn't mind seeing you. Anyway, your grandmother fixed me a 'snack' for the trip back, which not only lasted me three meals, but there's half of it left in the truck. Good thing, too, since I was broke."

"What did you do for gas?"

"You remember your Dad's credit card? Well, I used it. Think he'll mind?"

"He'll be surprised. And where is Big Horse? And how's it running?"

"Fine. I was able to bring it in closer than the mines. I found an old logging road that comes out on the river about five miles up. And that brings me to something else. I'm really tired, but . . . while I was out I called the teacher's college at Kingston. I've decided to go back to teaching, but I have to take a summer course first, for certification. We've been here a winter, and I see no reason to stay here, without money, without prospects, without even food. So, unless you can come up with some compelling reason, and I can't imagine what it would be, I think we should go to Kingston—I can float a loan for the summer, against a job in the fall. I'd like us to go together; but if you won't, I'm going anyway, and I'll come back for you in the fall. Well, what do you say?"

"What is there to say?"

"There's a lot of woods around Kingston. We don't have to live in the town. Glad to be back, darlin', g'night."

"G'night."

The next day we packed up and walked out, and as we walked out, the blackflies arrived. Burdened with books, cooking gear, sleeping bags, blankets, parkas, snowshoes, buckets, an ax, a rifle, the kerosene lantern we'd found, and the rotted tarpaulin, the last view I had of myself and of you in our wilderness children's disguise was of two fugitives from an unlikely Eden dragging themselves and their useless gear along an unused spurline, bothered by blackflies. And, next thing I knew, we were picking wild strawberries along the tidal flats of the St. Lawrence.

SUMMER

Ten

Kingston, Ontario, population (in 1963) of fifty-two thousand, is the site of the Royal Canadian Military Academy, the federal penitentiary (both women's and men's), and Queen's University. I was horrified at such an urban center, and at the prospect of renting a room—at fifty dollars per month, or maybe even seventy-five dollars so you could be near the college. Impossible! Driving around Kingston in Big Horse on a warm June day, a pleasant enough day in the country but close and hot in the city, I felt claustrophobic: the town, especially its harborfront on Lake Ontario's shore, weatherbeaten and seedy; the streets narrow; the houses squat; the rooms, up creaky stairs and through heavy doors, airless and squalid. We were shown and quickly fled from such a room, with plastic slipcovers on the sofa and a religious plaque over the flue. Hurrying down creaky stairs to a heavy door that let onto a narrow street, I had such a vision of the city as the city could scarcely comprehend: of people behind deadlocked doors in tiny airless rooms gasping under plastic, perishing.

"I can't," I said.

"Poor darling, it *was* small. We'll find a nicer place. We'll take another loan if we have to."

"I just can't," I said. "I'm not ready for the city. Let's find a place where we don't have to pay," I pleaded, "and where we can breathe, in the country."

"But it can't be too far. I have to drive into town every day, for classes. I have to dress. . . ."

We got in the truck and drove out of town, heading west past the city limits, then north through the next little village four or five miles away, Cataraqui. We were in country now, on a paved road flanked by ill-kept farms and ramshackle barns separated one from the next by unpruned fruit trees and lean dairy cows with reproachful eyes—the telltale holdings of men who commuted to work in the city. We passed two or three side roads, and at the intersection of a dusty concession with the main road, where a dirty-white stucco garage and wrecked cars sprawled on the corner, we turned. All very direct: as though this were the corner, and that the direction, and over the next hill, home. Now we were on a concession along which, at quarter-mile intervals, farmhouses fronted: not the desultory farms of part-time prison guards and mechanics, but the typical Ontario two-story farmhouses of sturdy red brick with graceful white trim at the gables; farmhouses that overlooked fields planted or fallow, but fenced, each house dominated by the unpainted barn facing it.

We passed one such farm, then another. At the end of a lane we spied a farmer at work in his barnyard, repairing a wagon. Without hesitation we turned down the lane and pulled up in his driveway, amid a fretwork of fences and barking dogs, between the house and the barn. And while I sauntered over to where he was standing, you sat in the truck and watched us, Lynn; for it was around seven o'clock in the evening, and the bugs were out, and the sun going down, and the swallows were swooping through the barnloft, from dusk to dusk through the darkness. You watched and waited resignedly for me to walk back and announce that we would spend the night under one of these trees, or drive on to find some other tree, as we had done every night since Mile 9. And as you sat on the truck seat and watched—the setting sun, the swallow barn, the farmer and me in the barnyard—the way the light fell on the old farmer you couldn't but notice his hands: the incongruity between his finely veined head on its long slender neck (he had on overalls) and his rough red hands, enlarged at the knuckles and thickened and horny with callus.

Then I came back to tell you that the farmer's name was Hooper and that we could camp in his field. And while Mr. Hooper walked on ahead in that long loping stride farmers have, driving his cows to pasture, we followed in the truck to a gate. From there we hiked with our gear to a spot out of sight of the farmhouse, bounded on one side by woods and, beyond, by a field of new oats. Our rotted tarp we spread for a groundsheet, and draped the windward side over a limb, then anchored the makeshift with rocks—of which Hooper's field afforded us plenty. And aside from an inquisitive cow in the night mistaking your hair for hay, and coming perilously close to wrapping his tongue around it, we slept in the field peacefully.

We lived there that whole summer (until late August, when a flash flood struck and we fled to the barn for cover), and the only black marks you received in your course work had to do with practice-teaching: not the lesson preparation, but your appearance—for your dress was never ironed, and your hair often tangled, but, by Christmas! you were working against odds. You were checked and counterchecked so often by bad weather, stymied and worn so by your struggle with the weasel, and so exhausted by your efforts to find wood and build a fire and cook breakfast, that when on dew-drenched mornings by sheer will and doggedness you managed to emerge from your lean-to in the back field (through the skirmish troop of cattle, and the trial of starting Big Horse) bearing not a mark of your daily "Battle of the Breakfast" but envying the birds their barn and the groundhogs their holes, then sometimes you were just too tired to brush the cockleburs from your hair. Yet all these difficulties you endured, of a wearisome, irksome, troublesome, unseasonably elemental summer; for all that, you prevailed—with me, with the school, with the weasel. You saw, while we were yet at Bartibog, whatever the nature of the tunnel we were entering, and however brief the privation, that we were not equipped and would need provisioning. And this equipping and provisioning, while making no demands on me, you set yourself to provide for us that summer. That you had to do so from a farmer's field and the cab of an old truck, rather than from the relative comfort of a rented room in town, was due to my aversion to the city; but you managed, sorry for nothing so much as that you could not accomplish effortlessly and without a show of strain what was virtually impossible to accomplish at all.

Our food, for instance. Ruth the Moabitess is said to have gleaned in the field until evening, and then to have beat what she had gleaned. But did Ruth, after she had gleaned and thrashed her barley, collect stones from the field with which to build a chest in which to store her grain, or get up in the night to repair her food chest from a weasel's depredations? Ruth wouldn't have liked Hooper's field.

Or take our shelter. The birds of the air had their barn-loft; the groundhogs had holes in the field; but we in our self-imposed hardship slept under a rotted tarp that wasn't rainproof, slung over a swaying limb. In time we battened it

down more securely, but when a heavy rain lashed the
canvas, we got sprayed and seeped upon, and when the wind
shifted to lee we got drenched. We tried several schemes to
keep dry and escape the bad weather, but really it was the
weather that drove us (as it no doubt drove primitive man)
into the shelter of three institutions: the library, the prison,
and school.

I have always respected libraries and librarians; they are
the storehouses of knowledge and the wardens of fame. Not
until the sixteenth century were books unchained from the
wall, and with the lending of books came the liberation of
man. Until the Reformation the only way to be learned was
to resort to monkery or magic, or, as Euripides is said to
have done, lock oneself in underground stacks for ten years.
Now a man can, with a library card that he can have for the
asking, explore the limits of knowledge with the greatest
minds of the past and bring light out of the darkness of his
own mind. And this, sitting in the map room of Queen's University Library, to which the librarian gave me a key—a safe
stronghold; a snug, warm spot; a haven from Hooper's field
—I set myself to do, while you, Lynn, sat all day in classes.

Here I would ponder, under the pretext of scanning *Paradise Lost* and needing quiet to do so, the baleful words of
the prophets in Hebrew, and a Greek grammar against the
day when I could read the Apostles' shining words. One
other book, which I cannot in conscience omit—for I encountered it after the Old Testament, and it determined my
approach to the New—was the Upanishads. The eleven classical Upanishads constitute the foundation scripture of
Brahmanism, Hinduism, and Buddhism, as the Old Testament does of Judaism, Islam, and Christianity. By a concen-
trated perusal of these two elder scriptures, I had by summer's end assimilated a religious yearning thousands of
years in the making, and one that for me the Christian Gos-
pels alone were capable of fulfilling.

But for the map room, in which I stashed raisins and nuts and burrowed myself every weekday, I wouldn't have been ready by winter for the New Testament. But even the map room didn't solve all our problems, for the library closed on the weekends. After one foul-weather weekend spent in the field—lying wet and cold and uncomfortable for the better part of two days and three nights—we contrived to get ourselves locked into the library the next Friday at closing time. We expected release Monday morning; picture our dismay, then, we who hadn't figured on a First of July holiday, on emerging bookwormish into the sun, blinking and hungry, a day late, a few years short of Euripides' record but nonetheless wiser in our resolve that some other contrivance for rainy evenings and weekends would have to be found.

And now occurred another of those uncanny coincidences that Christians attribute to God, but that almost always come to pass through human agency. The librarian, a Mrs. Humphries, who had been good enough to give me a key to the map room and so rescue me from Hooper's field, was also, it turned out, a member of some ladies' league, which supplied books to the women's federal pen and staged programs there for the inmates. One day she came to me (I was reading aloud in my map room—early Isaiah, I think—trying to sound like the roar of the sea) to ask if I would be interested . . .

". . . in giving a little talk to the girls?"

"Ma'am?" I laid Isaiah aside, face down, so that she wouldn't see the Hebrew; the league whose name she'd mentioned had "Christian" in the title, and I didn't want to take any chances on losing my map room. . . . "But what would I talk about? And who are 'the girls'?"

"They're all sorts, every sort, in for all sorts of things, and they do so appreciate . . . anything, Mr. York, anything with any content to it. Our regular Tuesday night speaker called to say, well, he had to cancel, you see, and . . . talk to

them about *Paradise Lost,* I'm sure they'd be interested. . . . Oh, and do come for supper, and bring your
lovely wife—downstairs, shall we say, at five-thirty?"

It is said of the Great Wall of China that it is not the wall
itself, but the *idea* of it that stuns one. For me it was the
fact of the women's federal pen: its high stone walls topped
with barbed wire and corniced with turrets and gun mounts
(count them: four); its maze of iron gates with square locks
and electric eyes (pass through and hear them clank shut
and click); its guards in uniform; its inmates in khaki; everything, in short, usually associated with a federal prison
(though when first I penetrated those bleak walls to "give a
little talk to the girls," it was a minimum-security prison,
which meant simply that the warden was liberal and the
guards were unarmed).

Mrs. Humphries introduced me to the warden, a woman
of about forty with iron-gray hair who assessed me quickly
with steel-cold eyes, decided I was harmless, and escorted
us to the messhall. On this occasion Lynn hadn't come, and
we entered the messhall, a huge room, which seated seven
hundred inmates—all women, of course, eating and smoking
and lounging, all in brown khaki outfits and silently, sullenly
staring. As we came in (Mrs. Humphries, the warden, and I)
and took our trays and made our way, excruciatingly slowly,
along the metal-and-glass cafeteria counter, seven hundred
pairs of eyes bored into my back, all of them staring at *me,* I
had such an image of myself as the electric eye would never
understand—of the diminutive male in a hothouse of flowers,
the flowers run riot with their roots and stalks tangled, giving off in the steamy gun-metal air a surcharge of oxygen
(or was it carbon dioxide?) so that one tried to breathe less,
but felt dizzy, as in a jungle. Then, after facing for twenty
minutes a mishmash of food that I couldn't identify, we
repaired through a labyrinth of iron gates and locked bars to
a smaller room, and before I knew it I had like the poet

been "thrustest into the middest" of my fascinating talk on
. . . I have forgotten what . . . seated on a chair in a circle
of a dozen rapt faces above khaki shirts with a sense that,
whatever else was being conveyed, the intensity in the room
far surpassed anyone's interest, my own included, in what
was being said. Then, as suddenly as it had begun, it was
over, the alarm had sounded, the girls were leaving, and I
was being led out—back through the gates, the guards, the
walls. Emerging into the foggy night with Hooper's field to
face, the prison by comparison seemed warm and dry and
secure, even comfortable, with food, lounge chairs, and listening girls—a captive audience. I was suddenly discon-
tented with the farmer's field and concerned to arrange a
follow-up talk, even a series.

So it was that for the duration of summer every Tuesday,
and then Tuesday and Thursday, and then every Tuesday
and Thursday and Sunday evening, we entered the walls of
the prison, and ate in the crowded messhall, and met with a
circle of girls who by the end of summer staged (though
none of them had ever acted before or made costumes or
scenery) a modest production of Synge's one-act *Riders to
the Sea*—chosen because it had an almost all-woman cast.
And while it is true that initially we were more concerned
with our own comfort than with the needs of the girls, it is
also true that through a summer of meeting together they
came to count on and trust us, and we came to know and
love them: the "Butch," in for life on a murder charge, who
would bring me each evening her ranting, rhapsodic poems
in which she pleaded with Death to come, and come quickly;
and Fern DeCarle, the lovely twenty-four-year-old from
Montreal (whom I insisted on thinking of as an Indian
maid, though she was really métis), who surcharged the
play's dialogue with her anguish at serving a seven-year sentence for drug trafficking; and Ruth Gavin, freckle-faced

and red-haired, from Vancouver, who joked that if ever the Mounties busted down her door when she *wasn't* taking a shower, she would go peaceably with them to jail.

Meeting three times a week with the same few girls over an entire summer, we came to feel compassion for them, though we had nothing to offer them except the play. And the play, and the numerous rehearsals of the play in which they poured out their stifled emotions, became, in effect, therapy sessions. When opening night did arrive, the stage set and the audience waiting, Fern got stage fright and wouldn't come out of her cell. She did, finally, and performed beautifully; then fled from the stage to her cell. It was the last time I saw her. My excuse for entering the prison was gone; Lynn's course was finished; summer was over.

The next day, sunny and cool, we took a walk through Hooper's fields. The oats in the far field were golden and ripe, the groundhogs lazy as they sunned by their holes, the cows no longer curious as they grazed in the pasture or stood chewing their cuds by the fence. You were feeling lighthearted and happy, flitting among trees in the ironwood grove, running and hiding behind big rocks, trying which ones could be moved; while I, inexplicably moody, scolded you. You didn't understand the significance of this—these rocks, those trees—I said; and placing myself beside a big boulder, I said it recalled me to God. You expressed surprise, said you would rather find God in the field of ripe oats or the cows. We argued, I calling your view superficial, you calling me grumpy and stern. And that was the first indication, that late summer's day in Kingston, of what was to become much more pronounced later—a religious strain in me that had more to do with ironwood and stone than with fields of ripe oats and milk. A sense of God in the rocks and the trees, but only the most immovable rocks and the most durable trees; of God at the basis of things—animistic, adamantine. And with it my feeling, amounting almost to a demand, that you, too, should take a much sterner view.

So that when you announced that you had taken a job teaching high school in Barrie, Ontario, I got angry. All I could see was that the quest, on which we'd only got started, was ended; that our search for the Self in which all unity resided had been sabotaged; and proof that we hadn't yet attained to Selfhood was that I had such feelings. As I stood by the stone in the ironwood grove, the words of the Isa-Upanishad darkened my mind:

> All who worship what is not real knowledge enter into blind darkness; those who delight in real knowledge, enter into greater darkness.

I saw myself as entering a tunnel, and, like a man in the grip of a whirlpool, grasping to pull you in with me. But you wouldn't come. The honeymoon was over, and you had your own ideas about what the marriage should consist of. If it wasn't to be all sweetness and light—ripe oats and sun and milk—it surely wouldn't be all sermonizing either—wet ground, cold nights, and Hebrew. So you stayed just out of reach, willing to concede anything—where we would live, how we would live, even our reason for living—provided your schoolteaching job was secure. And then you told me of the recurring dream you'd had. We had hitched a ride on a train heading into a tunnel, but there wasn't room for us, or for anyone, between the train and the tunnel—the passage looked suicidal—when suddenly you were on the other side, in the bleak waste and middle of a barren, burned land, seated around a campfire with a derelict group of survivors, waiting for the train to emerge. . . . I was on the train, and you were deathly anxious and afraid for me and discontent with the wasteland, without me.

Eventually, between ominous dreams and the advent of
autumn, a turn for the worse in the weather and the discomfort of Hooper's barn (for the use of which we had to help
out at haying), I reconciled myself to the impending move
to Barrie. We set out in Big Horse a week before you were
due, leaving behind us forever the rain-drenched field and
barn filled with new hay, which gave you allergic fits, passing the school where you'd practice-taught with disheveled
hair the whole summer, the Queen's University Library in
whose map room I'd spent my days, and the women's federal pen, where we'd taken refuge three nights a week. At
the outskirts of town, on an impulse, I pulled off the road at
a pay phone to call my parents—collect, of course—to tell
them where we were going, and why: the first news we'd
had since leaving the States which might give them cause to
rejoice. Mother on the line—

"Yes, yes, we'll accept the call." (Away from the receiver,
calling . . .) "It's Tom. Where are you, Tom?"

"How's everything, Mom?"

"Tom, your father's sick, he wants you to come home. He's
very sick, and the FBI has been here, Tom, it's awful, they
brought guns and handcuffs, and it upset your father.
Tom?"

"I just wanted to tell you we're moving to Barrie."

"Where?"

"It's in Ontario, don't have an address yet, but Lynn's got
a job there—"

"Tom, you must come home. Your father wants you home,
now. He thinks he can still fix things if you come home right
away. Are you near an airport?"

"Mo-ther! We can't just come home, just like that! Lynn's
got a job, and—"

"Here, speak to your father."

(A pause; a muffled sound—mother's hand over the receiver—and heavy breathing: my father . . .)

"Hello, son."

"Hi, Dad, how are you keeping?"

"Not too well. Can you come home, son?"

(Mother on the extension: "If you want to see your father alive, Tom, come home.")

("Now, Mother, I said I couldn't.")

He: "Well, whether or not you can, will you?"

I: (pause) "No."

He: (long pause) "Well, don't worry about it, son." (pause) "How is Lynn?"

I: "She's fine, Dad, fine. She's got a job teaching."

He: "That's good, she's a smart girl. Well, here's your mother—"

Then you took the phone, Lynn, because I was crying, crying like a little child in the phone booth, overwhelmed by the guilt and loyalty, the law and grace, the mortality and impossibility of it all. So we drove on to Barrie, and twenty miles outside of Barrie we camped—in a place, though we didn't know it yet, named Utopia.

THE SECOND WINTER

Eleven

Now, the way we found Utopia was this. We had driven to Barrie in Big Horse, and taken an apartment the same day—an upstairs room, with kitchen, like the ones we had been shown in Kingston and had rejected; but this one we took for two weeks so that Lynn could familiarize herself with the school prior to teaching, while I paced the room like a caged lion, went for long runs (five to ten miles) at night so as to be able to sleep, and tore around in the truck, a map clenched in my fist, from concession to concession and side road to side road, in a fit to find someplace outside the city where we could live.

One false lead on which we wasted some time (for I expected to locate a place, harum-scarum, as we had done at Kingston) was the pig farmer's place near Minesing. I had taken the highway west out of Barrie and passed through a tree farm, which seemed, as I passed it, to constitute a shield between me and the city; as I turned down the first

side road past the tree farm I fully expected to find my new
Eden. What I found instead was a pig farmer's hovel, half
dug-out, half concrete block, facing across a wallow in
which hogs were rooting a barn, the barn on the verge of
collapsing and sinking slowly like a stinkweed in the mire of
manure and garbage which the farmer, as brutalized as his
livestock, hadn't bothered to lime. A depressing sight, but
for some reason that I cannot now comprehend (perhaps
the resemblance of the place to that in the prodigal son par-
able), I offered the farmer, who lived with his blind mother,
my services around the hog wallow in return for permission
to build a shack somewhere on his property. He seemed suspicious, the more so when the next day I arrived with Lynn
and we traipsed his fields and woodlots in search of a site.
The farmer, fortunately, was so sunk in savage torpor that,
when we strode in from the field prepared to discuss things,
he merely grunted that it was feed time. We followed him
to the barn where lay a huge sow confined with her litter;
but when we went to pour the swill in, we discovered her
farrow all dead. She had rolled over on them, and crushed
them, and eaten the ones nearest her. We left the pig farmer
cursing the sow, and retired from the grisly scene and the
stench with the disquieting thought that he might, had we
been so unwise as to build on his land, have rolled over on
us and crushed us.

So it wasn't without blunders that we found Utopia; our
discovery of it wasn't coincidental with our arrival in Barrie,
as though we were nowhere one morning and now here that
afternoon. Our coming took time, for unlike those wise men
who are said to have traversed in twelve days what it took
us two winters to cross—the border, both geographical and
psychological, between what was not and what is—we had
neither star, nor astronomy, nor ancient faith for guide; but
we did have love, and one another, and restless desire goad-
ing us—and I driving wildly down side road after side road

searching for a concession block secluded enough on which to build a shack. For I had this idea, derived in part from the Upanishads, in part from the desert Fathers, that the journey psychological would begin when the journey geographical ended, and that to make oneself receptive to any signals from on high one had to place himself as far from all distractions as he could. *To live in the woods* was my sole objective at this point; just as, in order to dream, one must first sleep. So I drove on, and ignorance followed.

I came at last to a section bounded by the seventh and eighth side roads, by the tenth concession and Ivy Township road; the heart of the block, a fifty-acre tract of cedar swamp and rocky fields with a flimsy shack fronting the side road. The shack had been started by the owner of the land, a bankrupt businessman and, when we met him, a frustrated schoolteacher. He had dug a well, too—in a dry hole, on the wrong site, and, like the cabin he had started, left unfinished. It was here, near the abandoned shell of another man's dream, that our outward journey ended. We contracted verbally with our absentee landlord (who modeled his dealings with us on the ninety-nine-year feudal contracts he remembered from his boyhood in the Black Forest, before he had immigrated to Canada): to rent the plywood shelter for as long as it would take us to build a cabin deeper in the woods; and, in lieu of further rent, to leave all capital improvements (meaning the cabin we proposed to build) on the property when we moved on.

So now, in October of 1963, began a period of building deep in the woods, a mile from any road, the cabin in which during that winter of 1963–64 I was finally to determine for myself whether or not the words of the biblical Prophets had any power, the promises of the Apostles any substance, the meditative method of the sages any value—in short, whether or not the classical religious quest, entailing withdrawal from society, restraint of the senses, and concentration of the mind, still had, as according to Paul, Augustine, and Luther it once had, power to save. "For if ever a monk could win heaven by monkery," Luther wrote, "I must have done so." And likewise, if ever the walls of a house were called "Salvation," its rafters "Righteousness," and its roof "Praise," it must have been mine. I mimicked the beavers, and watched their lodge-building, before setting in on my own. I felt the smooth bark of beech-maple trees in selecting which ones to chop. I barked straight pine poles for the rafters, and split cedar shakes for the roof. And I notched the support gables of the sixteen-foot roof-tree in the form of a cross.

But many materials were needed for a sturdy, warm cabin —a many-windowed cabin, with much light—that it was not feasible to take from the woods around. Windows, a door, a sink, flooring and insulation, a stove—Lynn trucked these materials in from town after school, and I carried them in from the road. The path along which tortoiselike I carried these supplies led from the edge of the field (which, before snowfall, the truck could trundle over), across the stream by beaver dam, and through an overflow swale (choked with cedar roots and swamp vines), then up a small hill to a poplar ridge beside an old split-rail fence. At this point, a half mile from the field, I would usually lay down my load, catch my breath, and gaze at the sight before me: a great princess pine tree, shimmering in the sun, or spangled with raindrops, its huge drooping branches like skirts around its base, its delicate crown spiring forty feet above the other treetops. And past this princess pine and the open glade about it, I could spy the dark wood beyond: of dry and ancient cedar, heavy at the stump and densely foliaged at the top, so that a man could keep dry in a thunderstorm under its canopy. It was there, in that dark cedar grove beside the shining princess pine, that I set about building my wood shrine.

By early November I had the joists down and the floor laid, the walls up and the rafters on, and the shingles split for the roof. There remained only the cutting and barking of poles for the ceiling beams (the sixteen-foot gables comprised a sleeping loft, which made the room's ceiling eight feet), and the installation of windows and door. These tasks occupied me until mid-November. Still it had not snowed, and Barrie and the surrounding area I knew to be in a snow-belt, so I expected snow any day. Then, with the windows and door installed and the roof tacked on and ready for shingling, I gambled on the weather and brought in the sink and stove and other furnishings—but not without getting wet, for with the 250-pound "Quebec" heater on my back (which I didn't think I could lift, much less carry a half mile), I went through the beaver dam and nearly stumbled in the waist-deep water, but churned on and kept trudging, crunching more and more of the beaver dam beneath my feet and slowly rising, like a man mired down in fatness, from the bottom of the streambed to the bank. Without laying down my burden (for I feared I would never get it up again), I panted an apology to the beavers and staggered on, arriving with my brick-lined heater at the cabin feeling faint and just a few bricks short of a load.

We moved into the cabin in late November, before shingling the roof or installing the sink (which was simply for draining the water which was brought in daily by bucket; but Lynn insisted on a sink), before any of the amenities, such as insulation, were in place. Still no snow had fallen, and very little rain. The days were cool and crisp, the nights were cold, and every day without snow brought that lengthening of summer that in this latitude I deemed a miracle. But miracle is only natural event timed to the beholder. And by that definition our cabin was a miracle; for certainly a person entering our dark wood and thinking himself far from any dwelling, blundering noisily past the princess pine and stumbling unexpectedly into the cedar grove and spying suddenly the cabin, would think the sight of it miraculous. The denseness of the cedar grove and the nature of the cabin were such that, even if one looked for the cabin, it was not visible except from twenty yards or less; then, too, the many windows on all sides, which many birds flew into, and the roof of cedar shingles, added further camouflage. Miraculous—and I use the term advisedly—for I had two visitors that fall who thought it so.

The first was an RCMP corporal who had gone to Lynn's school that same morning, and ventured out to find me in the woods that afternoon. He came in along the path, which he found by means of a map Lynn had drawn for him, and normally I would have heard him or at least been aware of his coming, but I was taking a break from carpentering, as I did each afternoon, and was reading Scripture aloud—the Sermon on the Mount, I think—in the open space on the north side of the cabin. Striding through the waist-high withered grasses of last summer, open Bible in hand, I must have made a strange sight, inveighing the trees to take no thought for tomorrow, and the birds of the air neither to sow nor to reap nor to gather into barns, and the squirrels not to lay up plunder where moth and rust consume, or where thieves break in and steal. It was not posturing, but must have seemed so, had not the Mountie been all day looking for me, and only with great difficulty found me, and known that I had no warning of his coming. He stood in the cedar grove eavesdropping for some time, and the meaning of that word came home to me as slowly I became aware of him—an alien presence in the covert of the cedar, beneath the cedar-smelling eaves of the wood shrine. When I stopped reading he came out, with apologies for having interrupted me. He seemed a pleasant enough fellow, in plainclothes, and we sat down on a log nearby. He insisted that I read some more. When I had finished with the Sermon on the Mount, he told me who he was and what he had come for, and said he had two questions to ask me and hoped I wouldn't mind—he thought he knew the answers already, he said, but it was his job to ask.

I nodded, as much as to say "Go ahead."

"Do you intend to stay in Canada?" he asked.

Then, when I looked blank . . .

"Is it your intention to live in the woods here, in this cabin?"

In response to which I nodded gravely, as though to say like the planets in their orbits or the sun in its course, Venus and Mars might swerve from their paths, but not I.

"Do you intend to become a citizen of Canada?"

Again I looked blank, and was blank. It was not a question I had ever asked, nor one that, really, I was able to answer.

"What do you mean?" I said slowly.

"Well, just that, now that you reside in Canada, do you have any intention of becoming a citizen?" (Long pause.) "The alternative, though I'm not supposed to say this, would be to return to the States."

"No," I said, "I don't intend to go back."

"Well," he said, getting up and stretching, "I'm afraid I must. Wish I didn't have to, but . . . good luck," he said, putting out his hand.

And he was gone, toiling back along the path and over the stream and across the field, past the trees that took no thought for tomorrow, beneath the birds that neither sowed nor reaped. And the woods were left to quiet and to me.

I was still shingling the roof when our other visitor arrived, only this time it was the weekend, and Lynn was home from school and helping me. We were reveling in noise, both hammers going, while the woods resounded to our steady rat-a-tat. He appeared gnomelike in the clearing at the north side of the house, gaping up at us as at giants on the roof and at the life-sized gable in the form of a cross: a wizened little man, less than five feet tall and under a hundred pounds, his hands full of kindling—cedar sticks and birchbark—with a few frostbit, wormy apples propped on top like presents.

"She's l-l-like a palace!" he exclaimed. "Here, I b-b-br-brought youse somethin'," as he deposited his gifts. "You gonna l-l-live here?"

We allowed as how we were, and took a break, while Bobby Stringer gazed in through the windows like a child at a candy store. "It's p-p-posi-tively *dee*-vine!" he got out with effort, "live like a k-king here," he said, "an' a qu-*queen.*" And looking up at Lynn admiringly as she prepared to ascend the roof, "H-here, you shouldn't do that, l-let me he'p," he scampered up the ladder like a chimpanzee and blitzed through a section of the roof. He was certainly a worker, and a woodsman, and an alcoholic, and alone. He hadn't brought his dog with him this time, but had penned it in the tiny, filthy little metal shell of a trailer in which he lived, across a tract of maple trees, on the far side of the woods.

As we got to know Bobby Stringer better (for he was the only other person living in those woods that winter)—as we watched him pit his puny strength against giant beech and basswood stumps, digging trenches around their roots and chopping off their tendrils until he could burn them out and clear his five swamp acres; as we heard his stories of his drinking days, how he got started at age ten because he was a runt and was given liquor by the older boys and left dead drunk in a basket on his father's porch, the father who beat him, so that by age eleven he was a confirmed alcoholic; as we heard his stories of his drifting days, how one time he got religion on Manitoulin Island, when the Jehovah's Witnesses convinced him to get a job and give up drinking, and he did—got a job in a sawmill and kept a bottle beside him to curse at but never touched—and how after three days he had the shakes so bad that he cut off three fingers in a buzz saw, and while the stumps were still bleeding chug-a-lugged the whole bottle and then he felt better, and hadn't had a job since, nor religion; and as we came to understand how he came to be in his present position—picked up off skid row in Toronto and staked, in return for clearing some acreage, to a minimal shelter and meager supplies but with the chance of "drying out"—as we came to know Bobby Stringer better, we resented his presence in the woods less, and in the end we were even glad he was there, though Lynn was sorry she could do nothing for him. For we would sometimes hear him sobbing in the woods, and that would start his dog howling, and together they would make an awful racket—one that carried, on quiet starlit nights, across the buffer of a mile or more of dark woods and deep snow. But there was nothing we could do for him, though he did much, or wanted to, for us.

On this first occasion, though, he mainly gaped, and stuttered: admiring the workmanship of the cabin, which he found "el-el-elegant, f-fit for a k-king!" and the furnishings inside, which he thought "real p-p-posh!" And, indeed, the inside of the cabin was more elegant than the outside, for in addition to the sink and the brick-lined heater and the two single beds and easy chair we had purchased in town and brought in, there were the household items we had brought across the border in Big Horse: the green oriental rug Lynn's parents had brought back from Turkey, the feather comforters they had shipped out of Germany, the hand-made foot-stools they had bought in Yugoslavia; then, too, we had a kerosene lantern and a hurricane lamp, clothes (Lynn's prewoods wardrobe, around which we built a closet), and all the books we had collected as students at Tulane and later at Duke—an impressive array of accouterments with which to impress Bobby Stringer, and he was appropriately agog.

But the amenity on which he commented most was the primitive toilet I'd made. He didn't think a hole in the ground with two forked sticks supporting a pole was much of a latrine for a queen. "Might do for you or me," he mused, shaking his head profoundly, "but," and he looked around and threw up his arms in despair, "r-right out here, in the o-open?" Its primitiveness hurt his sense of propriety, and, strangely enough, like so many skid-rowers, vagrants, drifters, bums, and down-and-outs, he had a chivalrous nature, almost to the point of deifying the unapproachable female, or of making a cult of the virgin his one saving grace. Were it not so, and had it not bordered on religious grounds for him, I am sure he would have built a lavish outhouse for Lynn; but the mere thought of the function of such a building would have approached desecration. He preferred to shake his head and let such things be, and leave me, who had higher priorities in those waning days of autumn than woman's comfort, with his quaint caveat that my hole in the ground, while it might do for a king, wasn't fit for a queen.

What Bobby Stringer didn't know was that the queen of the manor was seldom home, anyway—only on weekends and evenings. Occasionally, too, she would overnight in town with the family of one of her students. The difficulty, each morning, of building a fire and cooking breakfast on a wood stove; of dressing in clothes washed by hand and pressed with a flatiron; then walking the half mile through wet underbrush, and struggling to get the truck started: all this before the day's work (which consisted of teaching Grades 9, 10, and 11 a subject she'd not taught before, English), Lynn found exhausting—especially after she started rehearsing a high school production of *Riders to the Sea* every afternoon after school, and found herself trudging home nights across the shadowy field, along the pitch-black path, to the primitive shack in the woods—too tired to prepare her lessons for the next day—then, as the days grew shorter, and the way home harder, her thoughts turned more and more toward securing a room near the school and confining her country excursions to weekends.

So the autumn days ran out one by one, clear and crisp, like sprockets clicking off a wheel, and everywhere in the forest roundabout were feverish anticipation and activity. The odor of ripe and rotten apples filled the open field; the scurrying of squirrels and chipmunks storing acorns broke the deep woods' hush, while a flock of evening grosbeaks in raucous raids at dusk, and a pair of speckled cedarlarks working steadily all day, vied with each other to denude the cedar grove of cones. In the open fields the bunch-topped elms, and along the fencerows cedars, and on the ground around my princess pine, leaves, fronds, needles: each signified that fall had ended, snow was coming, soon. While between forays to chop and cache wood, and sorties out to bring supplies in, as I contemplated the work of my hands, the wood shrine, I was grateful to the Lord of the Forest for having lengthened the season and withheld the snow, the purifying snow. For though summer was over, the harvest past, and still we were not saved, I felt confident of the winter coming on—that now that I finally lived in the woods, I would find peace like the snow, falling and everywhere turning everything into one face. And I said with the psalmist: "In the cool of these woods, in their shade, I will walk perfectly." And with Job: "Oh, when will my change come?"

Twelve

In the fall of that year, in the midst of a still afternoon, on Friday, November 22, 1963, at two o'clock, I did what I cannot remember having done before: I switched on the battery radio that Lynn had brought in to the cabin. The moving *largo* of Shostakovitch's Fifth Symphony blared out at me and compelled my attention—for was not Shostakovitch my favorite composer, and his Fifth Symphony one of my favorite pieces? The bittersweet, infinitely sad melodic line of violin and cello, counterpointed with horn and bass drum background—like the heavy tramp of marching feet through a sleeping garden—prepared me for the announcer's words that followed: "President Kennedy, who was shot less than an hour ago here in Dallas, has died on the way to hospital. I repeat, President Kennedy is dead. Already, expressions of shock and dismay are beginning to pour in from all over the world—"

Sudden as a shot and before snowfall, Death had entered the garden, had even insinuated itself into the woods where I lived. I stared out the window at the cedar grove, so still and so unstirred; I felt the glass not a medium but a protective shield—for the surrounding woods, which before had seemed a waiting venue of light, in a matter of a few moments had turned darkly ominous. I had tuned into the outside world for an instant, and Death was before me: in the branches of trees, in the leaves on the ground, in the neutral tones and the tortured colors, Death was before me now; so long as life was before me, so was Death. Then it turned dark and Lynn arrived, struggling in after a long day at school—over the beaver dam and through the vine-choked swale and along the path to the split-rail fence, before plunging down through the valley of shadow cast by the princess pine tree, from whose base she could spy under a dark brow of cedars the lantern glow in the window—Lynn arrived, having heard the news of death in Dallas, and bearing with her a letter from Little Rock:

Nov. 17, 1963

My dearest Tom:

I am very sad for two reasons. First, your Dad is slipping away fast. I shall take him to the hospital in the morning, because I can't feed him properly and he won't take his medicines. He is very feeble and I'm afraid he will fall when I'm not watching him. Just his presence here with me is very satisfying. I'm like Lynn, I am needed and have someone of my own, but this will end soon. The doctor gives no hope at all. He says the cancer is growing and that it is just a matter of time before it goes into uremic poisoning. Then your Dad will be in a coma. I'm sad for him because he doesn't realize anything. He knows me but doesn't say anything to me. The only reason I'm taking him to the hospital is so he can be fed intravenously and given blood transfusions. I will certainly miss his little kindnesses and his ways of doing things. I pray that he will not linger and suffer.

Now the other reason I'm sad is that my son is not here to be with me and his Dad. I understand your reasons, but am afraid you will have to come back under other conditions, and too late, then the regrets will all be in vain. The FBI agent called today to find out if we had an answer from you. I couldn't lie and you don't expect me to, so I told him, yes, you had answered, and were not returning. That's all I said except I asked him to please not contact Lynn's parents for they have no influence with you and she shouldn't suffer for your convictions. He assured me they would not get in touch with them at this time. Now, though, I fear that in spite of any assurances you may have from the authorities there, that you will be extradited. The agent said, "Now we will have to get him any way we can," so don't think the U. S. Government won't spend any amount of money, time, and effort to gain their point.

I am so sorry this is happening, though your Dad won't know it and it is only hard on me now for I really need you with me. This is a dreadful thing to go through all alone. I have no one. I am clinging to him now, trying to keep him here, knowing he should be in the hospital. Tomorrow I'll take my last tie to this place we love away from here, he is so sweet and trusting, but so sick. Well, I'm not trying to influence you, but wanted to tell you that you have been very foolish. Your Dad could have got you out of this, it's too late now, you have made your own decision. I love you very dearly and only wish you could be with me, and with your Dad. He'd still know you, but I don't know how long that will last. My best love to you both.

Mother

There was little I could do or say, and Mother was right in one respect: I had made my decision. So I continued to prepare for winter which, like Death, would surely come: chopping wood and caching it in great piles, building a sled with which to tow my wood come snowfall, and slaughtering with Bobby Stringer a ruptured ewe for stewmeat. This last event was one of the bleakest, most depressing acts I ever engaged in, for aside from the symbolic implications (of which I was painfully aware, and Bobby Stringer blithely ignorant), there was the bleating ewe, the yapping dog, the cursing man and, worst of all, the dulled and rusty knife. It was a hacking, sawing, harrowing blood-letting, not a slaughter, and when at last I had dispatched the gurgling creature with an ax, it seemed to me that all the land around had been so outraged and bloodsoaked that no amount of snow could cover it. My diary entries, too, from this interstitial period, postfall but prewinter, reflect a like concern: for purgation, purification, preparation before snowfall, and the illumination, if ever illumination was to come, that I was convinced would come with winter. I seemed to feel that all that ever was or ever would be could be present at one moment to the mind, provided the mind had been emptied, the senses restrained, and the self purged. To this end I directed my efforts, as these scribblings from the time indicate:

Nov. 24   Men have scourged their bodies because this was something they *could* do, a gesture they could make significant. The main point, as I see it now, is to cut out all indulgences. Because (1) every indulgence is its own reward: does not lead to something higher, but like labor seeks its rest; and (2) indulgences are distracting: divert man's energies from GOD.

Nov. 25   Not as an army marches, but as a tree grows, grows my soul. No doubt I am naïve, my sense of God extremely limited and, like a child's, conceited. Still, it's enough to instill in me, for the first time in my life, an overwhelming urge to better myself by self-discipline.

Nov. 26   God, as I perceive God, is not Outside or Other, but filling everything. Do away with the habit of thinking and speaking in terms of subject and object: by cultivating silence, and by the use of predicate nominatives. For example: sacrifice *is* self-pity, God *is* love; He *is* me, therefore I *am* Him. Try reading the Bible this way: "The Word of the Lord which came to me when I was with the herdsmen of Tekoa," or "The Word of the Lord which came to me by the River Chebar."

Nov. 27   "You must be born again" assumes a death, whereas the assumption of reincarnation is that there is one consciousness which adopts a variety of forms, no one of which is complete. The Buddhist must "remember births" in infinite regression; the remembered birth of the Christian is single and complete. "For the One who has become many remains the One undivided, yet each part is all of Christ."

Nov. 28   Alternate conceptions of God: anthropomorphic or ethereal. Less danger of ethereal conception being analyzed than of anthropomorphic being idolized. Old Testament very moralistic, ending in the wreck of morals on the cross. The Upanishadic way is to instill in the mind the sense and serenity of a perfect circle.

Serenity, the Circle *vs.* Passion, the Cross.

Nov. 29   What is this dark beyond dark? What is breath? What death?

Such searching questions, with which daily I ransacked my wounds, did not heal me; but they prepared me for the event I had long been awaiting, snowfall. Already I had invested snow with such meaning, associating its coming and the advent of winter with the bestowal of light from above, that I was bound to be impressed by the first snowfall. I had so long awaited it, and with such zeal prepared for it—in building the cabin, in cutting and caching wood, in slaughtering the sheep, and in constructing an icebox outside—that even a puny little snowfall of three or four inches would have given me a sense of completion. But in a snowbelt area such as the one I was in, much grander dumps were to be expected—up to two feet of feathering, full-bodied snow, which would cling to tree branches and cover fences and wood piles, and drift to a height exceeding houses and telephone poles. But what mainly I wanted to see, I think, was the snow on my princess pine tree. For just as I called the cabin my wood shrine, and the cedar grove my veranda, so I had made the princess pine tree my symbol, and the glade beneath it my holy grove. It was only about fifty steps from the cabin to the base of the pine tree—out the front door, through a little avenue of cedars, down a slight defile (which marked the end of the cedar grove, and the beginning of the glade around the pine), and up again, and one was under the protection of the outermost branches of the regal pine tree.

Here I would repair every morning. Awaking long before dawn, I would light the lantern and start the fire and sit down at the table—my breath frosting in the chill of the cabin, with mitts on my hands and a toque on my head and blankets swaddling me—to a couple of hours of the New Testament in Greek. Then, as the first faint light preluding dawn began to streak the forest, I would lace on boots and parka and set off out the door and through the grove and across the slight defile to post myself beneath the spreading branches of the great tree. Here, my back against its massy trunk, I would meditate: closing my eyes and standing,

loosely and relaxed, for a period each morning often exceeding an hour; for when I opened my eyes (and closed my
mouth: always, when meditating with my eyes lightly
closed, my jaw would gradually slacken and my mouth open
wider and wider until it seemed the breath within and the
air outside were one; then, when the meditation was over,
my eyes would open and my mouth close—this was my unfailing signal that the meditation was over), when I opened
my eyes I saw that the dawn had come and passed into day
. . . but the light of day was never so bright as the light
within. . . .

Then I would shamble back, like a spent shaman, all the
heat gone out of my body—from under the shelter of the
pine tree, across the narrow defile, and along the cedar
venue—to the cabin where, stoking the fire and melting
some ice, I would boil a potful of tea and cook a panful of
oatmeal. I always ate the same, I always did the same, at the
same time every day; and in this unvarying and unthinking
routine each day unfolded securely and serenely. There was
only the one defenseless moment, when on my way to the
pine tree I crossed the open defile (it was perhaps six feet
across and four deep, but gently sloped and carpeted, like
the rest of the forest around, with mosses and ferns)—that
one moment only, between the security of the wood shrine
and the sanctity of the grove, I came to dread, and Lynn did
too; for on those few occasions when she would get up to ac-
company me, she balked at that point and turned back.
Later on, I understood; for it became for me too, as my
meditations under the tree became less conscious and more
intense, a place of indecision, the point at which as I passed
through I asked myself if I truly did wish to discover what
was soon to be revealed.

Thirteen

The day began as had the days preceding it: the neutral-toned and uneventful days when no snow fell. The dawn I greeted at my princess pine was no ruddier than usual, the morning frost no more brittle, the air no more keen. By noon, when I left to chop wood and fetch ice, the sky was beginning to curd; I could scent in the air a thickness, a closeness, as if, deprived for a season of fire and water, air was descending to earth. The blows of my ax thudded dully, without resonance. By midafternoon I was back at the cabin; the sky had turned gun-metal gray, the air chill. Even the brown upside-down bird, which clung to cedars and traveled down tree trunks all day, had flown off. The woods were dark and deathly still, the woods creatures were waiting, hidden and hushed, for what would surely pass.

We sat on the bed, I remember, and watched the first few flakes feather down aimlessly from a snow-laden sky. Then the air outside was filled with snow falling, and we made love. Afterward you went to sleep, while I went out and stood—without my cap, without my coat, feeling the cool, wet, clinging flakes on my face and arms and thinking . . . nothing, nothing at all—just feeling, feeling warm and dry and free.

Some feelings are forever: death is forever, and love is forever, and snow . . . the first snowfall is forever, like the first love, primal and perfect, its lesson unrepeatable, its imprint true; it covers what before was naked and unknown, lonely and ignorant, and clothes with knowledge all it covers, the knowledge that in love, in death, all is one body from which none escapes, in which all breathe and creep and fly, to which all must submit—for everything that lives in love is lovely, deadly, deadly-lovely, buried for a season beneath snow. . . . I stood, and stood a long time in the feather-dusting snow, in darkness so immense and silence so serene it seemed that millions of voices were hushed and cities darkened, still I stood . . . awaiting what more permanent than snow I could not say, nor who more loyal than you, Lynn.

Fourteen

In December of that year, Lynn left. The snow was deep, the days were short, the path to the cabin across the stream and through the woods nearly impassable. She took a room in town closer to school, and she flew home to North Carolina for Christmas. Now I was left alone, alone as I had always said I wished to be; I saw no one, I spoke to no one, and no one spoke to me. My daily routines had by this time become rituals: up in the morning before dawn to read in Greek the Gospel of John; meditating by the first light beneath the princess pine tree; then, after breakfast, the mornings spent studying the Upanishads, the afternoons out in the forest chopping and sledding in wood. I supped each night on mutton stew, which I made at each week's beginning; fetched water in a five-gallon bucket from the stream where I kept the ice broke; and by lantern light read the Prophets in Hebrew before going to bed. My sleep was always sweet, and my reason unclouded.

Throughout this time, while I was reading John's Gospel, I was concerned with the place of Christ in my quest. Already I had experienced frequent mystical transports, as well as deep trances—while walking through the snowy woods, while reading the Upanishads, but mostly while engaged in meditation—but none of these lapses or releases from my normal conscious state could by any strict interpretation be called "Christian," any more than an end-of-the-world dream could be called "prophecy." For while dreams and prophecy had certain elements in common, I was convinced by my reading of the Bible that prophecy did not occur in solitude; nor, I suspected, did Christ appear, however pleasant the transport or deep the trance, in the guise of impersonal Nature. I was grateful for the heightened awareness that, morning after morning, was granted me; I only questioned where it all would lead.

My diary entries from the time reflect this concern to fit Christ in, or at least to make room for him:

Dec. 17   Sight for day, hearing for night. Dawn and Dusk, periods of transition, demand both sight and hearing, and strain both. If ever Christ should appear, it would be at dawn or dusk: as in the garden to Mary, or on the road to Emmaus. Dawn and Dusk the best times for meditation.

Dec. 18   Meditation: not a fixing or settling of the mind on any one object or idea, nor a flitting from one to another by way of association or remembered event; but by holding all in abeyance an awareness of all occurs, short-circuiting thought and language. Have reached through meditation a state of identification with and compassion for all living creatures. Is there a God beyond?

Dec. 19   Christ stands in the way of all who have a will to power, crying "I am the way!" To teach the proud humility? He mediates between God and the downcast, but for the discontent and strong of will he bars the way.

Dec. 20   I record here two experiences, both within the past month, which I shall call trances to distinguish them from my daily meditation. Even intense meditation, entailing identification with the cold (in which state I feel no cold, though lightly clad in sub-zero temperatures), I can control, bring on and shake off at will; whereas trance sweeps over me, is not self-induced, is more complete and more serenely powerful. Indeed, is bliss. When you come out you are merely thankful, nothing else, at having been allowed to encompass all pleasure and pain.

Dec. 22   Prayed to the Lord today to tell me what to do. It is obvious that I have experienced illumination, but not union. Also, that I am frightened at the prospect. What I know already is terrifying enough. To realize *that* . . . !

Then, around the turn of the year, several breakthroughs occurred in the ongoing struggle to void my mind of acquired patterns of thought, especially the tendency to think in dualistic terms, such as subject and object, mind and body, I and other, etc. I knew—instinctively, I think—that the only way to come at God was to live as the mystics had: as if only God existed, only God and me. This I had attempted to do by simplifying my life and ridding myself of concern for others who, whether father or mother, wife or FBI agent, were all essentially like me, so that concern for them would not make me other than I already was. But One did exist, I was convinced, who was sufficiently different; so much so that, as Pascal put it, "Compared with the infinite, all finite things are equal." But, having now arrived at that impasse—the confrontation of the infinite (I Am) with the finite (me)—what was I to do? I was still locked in a dualism, without power or intelligence to get around or break through. Not for the first time, certainly, but as pathetically as ever, the puny individual stood before the all-powerful absolute, longing for an encounter. Would I be crushed? Or simply ignored? Had audience ever been granted? And if so, for what purpose? I, of course, was convinced that it had and, if I chastened myself sufficiently, that it would—not automatically, or impersonally, but mercifully and compassionately, as a seeking father might receive his prodigal but repentant son.

The first breakthrough occurred in early January. Just as the releases I had experienced in meditation and trance gave me the sensation of being freed from time and space, so this conscious intuition involved the unshackling of my mind from the I-Thou impasse in which I had languished. And since the I-Thou relationship constitutes a fairly sophisticated dilemma, which few who have attained it have considered a limitation, I should say that, had I not been struggling toward Christ, I would have been content to remain there, for its dialogue was comforting, and its content certain—like deep calling to deep. But there was something less than personhood involved in either party, the stress was all on the relationship; and I felt then, as I feel now, that relationships didn't matter, persons did. So I pressed on to the Speaker of the Word, still shrouded in darkness. Again, had I at that time been familiar with Pascal, I might have broken through in Christian terms; for Pascal, in the same impasse, says: "Knowledge of God without knowledge of man's wretchedness leads to pride. Knowledge of man's wretchedness without knowledge of God leads to despair. Knowledge of Jesus Christ is the middle course, because by it we discover both God and our wretched state." But I hadn't read Pascal then, and I didn't feel wretched.

I felt confident, expansive, rapturous, serene—anything but wretched. I did not exult in human pride, and I was not especially humble. I saw myself as a student dedicated to learning—and if a man devotes himself to learning, shall he not be taught?—at the feet of an unseen teacher whose hieroglyphs were everywhere, and whose lessons were before me: in the spreading rose of dawn, in the restful hush of dusk, in the changing of the seasons, and in the realizations that visited me morning after morning through meditation and the books that were my study.

I had reached the point in my reading of the Upanishads where Brahman, or the Self, is revealed to the student as food: "Let him never abuse food, that is the rule; let him never shun food, that is the rule; let him acquire much food, that is the rule." This reverent and right regard for food having been established, the concept is expanded vertically: "There is food, and there is the eater-over-food; and he who is this food in man, and he who is that eater-over-food in the sun, both are one." Having realized this, the student completes the lesson by singing: "I am food, I am food, I am food! I am the eater-over-food, I am the eater-over-food, I am the eater-over-food! I am the poet (who joins both together). . . . He who gives me away, he alone preserves me: him who eats food, I eat as food. This is the Upanishad." It was in these terms, then—the reduction of everything bodied (and thus perishable) to food, and of God to not only the giver of food but also the eater of it—that I broke through the subject-object dichotomy that had been stymieing me. My statement of the solution took the form of a sonnet, which in some strange manner expressed my way around the impasse:

> This is food also, this is the true food:
> Which if you eat, you never again hunger;

But if you refuse to eat, you hunger
Ever after it, for who denies this food
Denies the eater-over-food. No food
Will satisfy when comes upon him hunger
After life lost and insatiate hunger
After more, but the eater-over-food:
He it is provides your wherewithal, who
Feeds you of himself; he also gnaws
And feeds himself, he feeds himself on you—
Who else? And he who knows this, because
He eats and was eaten of this hymn,
He eats all, and all they have, and they eat him.

God-who-was and I-who-wasn't were no longer separate and distinct entities, deep calling to deep, little deep wailing to great deep for a bridge across the chasm; both were food and both were eaters, both organic, and both intimately bound—God to reveal himself, I to reflect his revelation—as, in the process of star formation, light results when gravity is released from collapsing matter. And if God, like gravitational force, was a circle whose circumference was nowhere, and whose center was everywhere, then the time and the place, the delay and the setting of what was soon to occur, were dependent solely on me, on my readiness. So I began an attempt to consecrate every action, and every task I performed, to God; to maintain a constant consciousness of the whole, while performing automatically and ritually the parts of my service. But in this I was mistaken: I had got too wrapped up in my own methodology (which had worked thus far) and too carried away by my own spirituality (which seemed to me spotless) to come any closer to God. For not only would God, or the Beatific Vision of God I seemed to be seeking, not be coerced, but also I had yet to break through a far more human dilemma before my mind could be emptied and my spirit humbled enough to let

Christ in. There were, after all, fear and cunning, guilt and shame, in the woods as well as in the world. Utopia was a pleasance and the site of my spiritual quest, but it was also the name of a rural mail route in southern Ontario.

Fifteen

The woods were still that Wednesday, the winter sun was bright, and I had just finished my morning meditation beneath the princess pine tree and was standing, quietly blending into the background of which I was a part, when he burst into the clearing on the far side of the grove—huffing and puffing while smoking a cigar and carrying a double-barreled shotgun. He trudged across the clearing loud as a hunter at noon, his big boots crunching through the crust of the snow, a big man, one who could have played St. Nick, clad all in red: red hunter's jacket; red hunter's cap with ear flaps; and, behind the puffs of cigar smoke like blasts from a locomotive, big ruddy face. Without a moment's reflection he plunged headlong into the cedar grove beside the cabin, then stopped. I watched him scrutinize the cabin, walk around it, peer in and look around—still he did not see me— then proceed more circumspectly through the grove and across the little dip into the glade where I was standing. I stepped out from the pine tree to meet him.

When I stepped out from the shadow of the tree to meet my visitor that morning—an overweight angel disguised as a hunter, puffing a cigar—I had nothing particular in mind, was not expecting company, neither saw nor looked for any sign of recognition. I had read, of course, of the angels who had visited Abraham and Lot, of the angel who had come with weeping news to Joshua, of the angels God had sent to paradise to instruct Adam, but I didn't associate those visitations with this one. Nor did he. He was as surprised to see someone as I was, and we never even exchanged names, never shook hands. But as soon as we had met and conversed for perhaps five minutes—after which he trudged on —I knew without a doubt that he had visited me in God's stead; and queer though the notion may seem, I think he thought so too.

The first thing we established was that he wasn't a hunter, carried no shells for his shotgun, and that this wasn't the first time he had ventured from his home in Toronto for a tramp in the woods in midwinter. As for these particular woods, and this particular grove, he had spotted "Utopia" on the mailbox and stopped his car and walked in. He wasn't sure where he was, but he wasn't worried about finding his way back. He certainly wasn't looking for anyone, and was surprised to find the cabin. But after we had established all that, and after I'd asked him if he would have tea, and he wouldn't, as I walked with him to the edge of the field, we talked, and he spoke without guile the words I had been waiting to hear.

"I can see," he said, "that you're a man far better educated than I am—"

"Oh no," I said.

"Oh yes," he said. "I can tell by the books I saw through the window, and by the way you talk. It doesn't matter, though. More important, you have a strong conviction of God—"

"That's true," I agreed.

"And you love nature, and you're extremely independent. Now, what I want to know is this"—he had stopped walking to face me—"Are you preparing for the ministry?"

"The ministry?" I echoed vaguely.

"Because if you're not, you should be. You've reached a point now where you should begin considering others. By the way, are you married?"

"Are you sure you wouldn't like a cup of tea? It wouldn't take long," I demurred.

"I'm sure. Where is your wife? Does she live here with you?"

"She lives in town," I said. "She teaches. Lately I've been thinking of attempting a year of silence. I guess she finds it dull here."

"A year of silence! Listen, life's so blinkin' short you mightn't be here next year—none of us might! Anyway, you're not free to be silent, or chaste, or poor, or alone— you've got a wife. What will you do when children come?"

"Children? We've only been married a couple of years—" I trailed off.

He looked at me as if to say, "You may know some things, but you're certainly ignorant about the basics." "Well, whatever you do, don't quarrel with your wife, don't make her unhappy. She's your first responsibility."

"My first responsibility is God."

"Don't worry about God. God can take care of Himself. He's taken care of you, hasn't He? You do for your wife as God's done for you, and once you've done that, consider the ministry. The ministry needs men like you."

Then, relighting his stump of a cigar, which had gone out, he trudged off across the field, his big upper body bent forward, his ruddy face thrust ahead, his double-barreled shot-

gun poking the snow as he went and kicking up little glitter-
ing sprays of snowdust into the smoke puffs he left behind.

All the rest of the day I was moody and morose, pondering what he had said. It seemed to me I had reached a dead
standstill, got caught in my own cunning trap. For I was engaged in a desperate struggle—flight my only credentials, my
only achievement exile—away from the dark warm wet
mother-earth, toward the light dry cold father-spirit: nature
was not sufficient for me, nor anything less than pure mind.
And in this quest which had brought me North away from
all that I cherished and dreaded—the decaying South, my
father's deathbed, even the love of Lynn—I was balked by a
specter nearer to me than my own shadow, an enemy I
could never make peace with, for however far or fast I ran it
would always run with me, within me. I might call it by various names—Death, the World, my own Body—but whatever
I called it, however I fled it, the energy expended in scourg-
ing myself and in holding myself aloof from it (and from all
it tainted and overtook—from society, family, Lynn—from
everything human and fragile) was sufficient to prevent me
from attaining the spiritual union I sought. I had reached
the point at which Augustine, Luther, George Fox—indeed,
all whose yearning to merge with God was also a desire to
make themselves godlike—at the height of their asceticism,
were forced to acknowledge the ultra-moral as anti-life, and
thus immoral, and all their self-denials as constituting a mechanical assault upon God. For, certainly, that is immoral
which interrupts energy flow; and God, if He came not to me
as naturally as the leaves to the trees, or ice to the stream,
had better not come at all. Any other coming would be
forced, and since God could not be coerced, a starvation vision would be as suspect as a drug-induced trance—a projec-
tion of my own troubled thoughts rather than a divine visitation.

Such, more or less, was the morass in which I was floundering. Then, in the midst of this wallow of self-doubt and distrust, with the black hole of space yawning before me, my cigar-smoking angel had visited me to correct, somewhat, my crooked perspective. And what he had said, as I mulled it over, was that whether or not there was a light at the end of the tunnel, there was an end to the tunnel. This passage I was engaged in had a name; it was called conversion. And there was a support group gathered at the end to receive those who came through—the Church. The success or failure of my quest didn't matter; what did matter was that I believed in God enough to search for Him. Let every troubled person, caught in the snare of his own or another's cunning, pinned in the pit of the deadfall that breaks humanity's back, ponder these shining words: "In him was life, and the life was the light of men. The light shines in the darkness, and the darkness has not overcome it."

That same night I had a dream, which troubled me so on awaking that I couldn't concentrate on the Scriptures until I had written it down. As often occurs, the dream was in three interlocking parts.

I was at an outdoor country dance, dancing with a woman (Lynn) who had two holes, like bullet wounds—one in her neck, the other through her breast—which were slowly bleeding. I danced very close to her so that no one could see the wounds because they might think I'd killed her, but kept being cut in on, and finally yielded her to a heavy-set fellow (Death). To my amazement she danced the entire dance with him, quite vivaciously, like a mechanical windup toy. Then, without warning, a cataclysm struck the entire dance party—all fled—a pileup of bodies at the end of the floor. I scrambled over them and escaped with one other survivor.

The other survivor and I are watching a movie in which Death stars, but serialized, so that between this and the next strip we return to our graduate studies in a castlelike library. The librarian leads us up to a room in which our books reside, but in which also Death sits. The end of our studies is to know precisely who Death, who sits watching us, is.

Mother and Dad and I on the farm outside Little Rock. I am considering selling Goldie, the heifer I raised from a calf. Death comes to buy her; he is a heavy-set fellow with a wide-brimmed hat standing between the garden and the milkhouse in the rain. I take out a raincoat for him, but he has one on already. He moves toward the house and lets himself in. Dad is confused before him, ill at ease. Death just stands there, with his hat on, unyielding. The calf gets loose and I run after it, trying to catch it for Death. Then I am chasing a greased pig.

This Dance-of-Death dream set me to wondering whether I hadn't always been obsessed with and fearful of Death, and whether there weren't some way to directly confront Death, rather than running from Him. Even in isolation I seemed to be surrounded by hostages to fortune who, as one by one they became Death's victims, joined in Death's dance. I was always outside (this was my dilemma): the survivor of a field of slaughter so encompassing, so universal in scope, that my survival (or anyone else's) was a mockery.

I was still maundering about this problem, which had to do with life's wholeness, and wondering whether any change, even the great change, Death, could destroy the fabric of wholeness, when by the first faint light I left the cabin and passed among cedars and paused at the edge of the grove. In the early-morning stillness, day, or its suggestion, cast a cold eye on the frozen forest. No sound yet, no sight, not even the muffled rustling of birds, or the unfolding fingers of dawn. Behind me the cabin, in which I felt so secure, stood stricken with blindness and dumb, a dark blob huddled in fog in the dense cedar thicket. Before me the princess pine stood, its massy trunk rising out of the mist, its bushy top blending into blind darkness—a single brush-stroke.

> All who worship what is not real knowledge, enter into blind darkness; those who delight in real knowledge, enter into greater darkness.

I crossed the slight defile dividing the grove from the glade and entered my appointed place of meditation at the appropriate time. Taking my place at the base of the pine tree, I wondered where, if anywhere, it would all lead: the Dance of Death, the quest for Life, the passion and the dream of these two winters. Slowly I closed my eyes . . . the dawn outside was spreading now . . . and slowly my mouth opened . . . growing more and more distinct . . . the woods around me slowly woke as rhythmically I breathed. . . .

> . . . somewhere between sleep and awakeness yeastily surveyed the rime-cold globe below through yeasty eyelids. Nothing moved before this, nothing was. He drowsed awhile hoping to remember . . . but his warm awaking breath lapsed not but iced his eyelids yeastily. Sometime below him desolate dark lay the stand-still earth, a weird place without heat; the subject void round him was, in him and around her. He moved a little nearer, then sunk back: whatal he wished all seemed to him within him, half-forgot; he moved again. . . .

I was still deep in meditation, but not sunk in trance, when where it would all lead, and who would lead me there, became as clear to me with my eyes closed as day to the woods creatures.

January 30, 1964

> Jesus appeared to me, and I saw with my eyes closed, against a glowing background of red light, the dawn

outside, and He stood in the upper left-hand corner, and came from the left side, and stood, and stood a long time, waiting; but I doubted, but rehearsed to myself over and over: "It's not you, Lord, I doubt, but I doubt myself, that this vision is true." For I had heard, prior to His coming, "Until you leave the surface of things, you will be blind." These words repeated themselves until the red light formed, until He came. Then He came more toward the center, down and from the left; He began stabbing a dead tree that stood before Him, gouging at it with His carpenter's tool; He continued hollowing the tree out with His hands, and scooping out the dead wood with His hands while I looked on, wondering, but He kept on; until at last when the hole was big enough, He stopped and while I wondered and stood considering what He might do with it, He stuck His head inside it, looking up (the tree, which I suppose was hollow), then drew Himself in and up, His whole body He drew inside and up into the tree, till He was lost to sight: signifying that He would be hidden in the earth a season, and be lost; whereupon the words,

> "Come, O Dithyrambus,
> Enter this, my male womb,"

came to me.

The imagery of the vision was not veiled to me, nor capable of nor even requiring interpretation. I knew, immediately upon perceiving them, the dead tree for the world, and Jesus for Jesus; I was permitted to witness what He did with the world; what I would do was left to me. There was no compulsion, no constraint, no command; merely example, and invitation—to enter the dead trunk of the world, as He had done. And there was a promise implicit in the invitation: because He was who He was, and had done as He had, and had not died (as proof of which He now appeared to me), so I, should I do as He did, would perish only for a season, as He had. The words of invitation with which the vision ended I had never heard nor seen before, but I had been reading Greek, and subsequently I came across a similar invocation in the *Bacchae* of Euripides, taken, probably, from the rites of the Greek mystery religions that flourished around the time of Christ.

I turned from the princess pine tree that morning neither ecstatic nor troubled, neither nostalgic for what had passed nor anxious for what would come. The quest was ended, all passion spent. Night and Death had fled from the woods: birds were chirping, squirrels were chiding, a chain saw buzzed in the distance. Day had come, and work was before me.

SPRING

Sixteen

Now time must pass. For, except for the death of my father, and our entrance into the Church, nothing significant happened to us as that winter passed into spring. The soul's dark night was behind me, my conversion complete, and the light of day at the end of the tunnel made plain what was to occur: gradual withdrawal from the woods and spirited return to the world. There were no further trances, visitations, visions. I had found my vocation through what I had undergone; my concern now was that others come to know Christ: first Lynn, then the friends we had made (at Bartibog, Kingston), the Church we had joined (in Barrie), and, finally, cost what it may, the society from which we had ventured. But for that last encounter, the U.S.A. *v.* me, the time was not yet. I wasn't yet ready nor, really, equipped to do something *that* crazy for Christ.

Besides, I was an eccentric—part nature mystic, part zealot—whose rustic habits and rank smell and sheer intensity put people off. Not that people regarded us as more strange than they had before, but we regarded people more: the woman in the Bible study group in Barrie at whose invitation we stayed overnight, who refused to give us a blanket because it would smell like the sheet (of woodsmoke and sweat) and be harder to wash; or the students from Lynn's class who visited us at the cabin and found us "weird"; and one English teacher (he later lived with us in Toronto while I attended seminary) who found it incredible that a person who had scanned Milton could actually believe with such "zeal"—than which, as Swift rightly remarks, a more pejorative term was never coined. Even Peter Taylor, who had initially found the cabin at Bartibog for me and put Lynn on the train in Moncton, when I visited him and his new wife in Ottawa that February—even Peter found me hard to take. I returned from that, my first trip away from the cabin for more than a night, dispirited and dejected. Upon returning, I recorded in my diary:

> Feb. 18   How desolate is the wood shrine, all warmth gone out of her. I had been away ten days, and all warmth left her.
>
> It is wrong to leave a house, and the birds and squirrels and creatures that depend on her; even though you go on the Lord's business, it is wrong. A fox killed our tame rabbit, and many birds have flown away.

Throughout these months between the vision (January) and our first mission field (June), it was Lynn, mainly, who bore the brunt of my zeal; for, confined to the woods as I was still, I was moving with great force on a very small floor: bludgeoning everyone about me with the sword of the Word—and, for the most part, everyone was Lynn. What I was demanding of Lynn at this time, when on the weekends she visited me, was (of course!) that she quit her job and come live in the woods and meditate as I had. And how I ra-

tionalized to myself this new trial for Lynn was as follows. From our plantation days in North Carolina, through
our woods life in northern New Brunswick, the summer
spent outside Kingston, and now here in Utopia, I had forever wanted to be left alone and always pushed Lynn to the
side; though, in fact, she was always beside me, as near me
as Nature was near—working, nude, in her garden at Durham, snowshoeing around Bartibog, on fishing jaunts at Mile
9: forever wresting a living from Nature, supporting me.
Hadn't that been what had led us to Kingston and brought
us to Utopia?—a larger garden for Lynn to work, so that I
could study and read? And now that what was to have happened, had happened, our quest come to an end, I was
released from my studies; but Lynn was still working. . . .
So what did I do? What anyone whose mind has grown stale
from solitude and whose reason has been riddled with visions would do: demand that she quit her job! It was this
demand, when I mentioned it in a letter home, that evoked
my father's last protest:

February 29

Dear Tom,

By what right allwise or otherwise do you presume to
play God with the lives of other people? And since
when do the spiritual attainments of life require that
one quit work? You seem to be trying to convince everyone to quit their jobs and throw themselves on the
mercy of the Almighty.

I submit that it may well be possible that your call be
garbled in the reception thereof. Why should you place
an additional burden on God to help you first before
you can help other people? You say you plan to live "by
faith alone," but doesn't this really make you dependent
on someone for your actual worldly existence? Your
thinking it necessary to force yourself into privation for

spiritual development is not so bad, but to drag others with you does not seem to me anything other than selfish.

At the time of Christ a man did not reach his majority until he was 30 years old. I realize that no one likes to be called too young for mature thought and consideration, but may I caution you that your enthusiasm, a marvelous attribute, may also be a two-edged sword. If you are serious, and I guess you are, and wish to devote your life to saving souls including your own, it seems to me you should first prepare yourself to do so. Get ordained, don't go off half-cocked, which you are prone to do.

Your last letter is disturbing. You would have Lynn quit her teaching before the end of the school year. For what possible legitimate purpose? "To save what's left of her soul." Aren't you playing God again?

Love,

Dad

My poor father, in and out of hospital, summoning his last energies to protest my latest caprice—what a failure he must have thought himself as a father when he considered his only son, me. And poor Lynn, trudging out tired on the weekends, after a hard week at school and lonely nights in a cheap boardinghouse, to a Spartan regime of hewing wood and fetching water and, worse, enduring me. "Better never to have come to Canada!" she might have wailed—but she didn't. As week after week passed in this fashion, it became apparent even to me that, with my energies released from the quest that had ended, and nothing better to do than lay in wait for Lynn on weekends, I needed some outlet, some plan. For if Lynn really were to quit her job, and we to live in the woods, there were economics to think of. The slaughter of the ewe might be a once-for-all act, and I and food might be one, but my mutton stew wouldn't last through spring. So it was that as the unconquered sun turned more and more toward the east for its rising, and took longer and longer to traverse the sky, I turned my thoughts to the maple bush and, with Bobby Stringer's help, took to attaching bails to gallon cans and whittling wooden spigots.

By the beginning of March I had about forty spigots and pails, so many that the entire sleeping loft of the cabin was covered with them. The strong spring sun each day was beginning to melt the fields and to make slush of deep drifts by the fencerows, and the slush would crust over each night. Each morning I had to arise earlier to get in my Greek before dawn, and each evening I went to bed later. Days were brighter, nights were briefer, dawns were glorious, and everywhere throughout the forest the sap was beginning to rise. On March 12 I watched a sleek brown otter slink through the cedar grove, rubbing his back against tree trunks as he went, changing streams. On March 13 I recorded: "A glorious spring morning! Light, which as a pale rose blossoms rose the dawn: pink petals spreading, then the heart shed," and I asked myself: "Does a rose have a center? And even if so, aren't its petals and their spreading so conjoined that the parts of its unfolding cannot be considered partially? So may my life exfoliate to God." On March 14 spring assailed my senses, wafting odoriferously up from the swamp to high ground. I trudged through the mud in which frogs were still burrowed, and plucked a marsh marigold. Then, on March 15, a Sunday, I left early and walked the twenty miles to Barrie, met Lynn there, and went with her to church. Every time we attended church, which wasn't every Sunday, we encountered the same Spirit whose presence I sensed in the woods—an abiding presence that could never be diminished, never die. After church, and a light lunch in Lynn's room, I walked the twenty miles back home, cutting crosslots and through fields and over fences, until I approached my maple bush where the trees were beginning to run. And striding through the maple bush to my wood shrine and secluded grove, hearing ducks call in the distance and flushing a flock of grosbeaks, I felt so intensely grateful—for the woods, the birds, the day—that I had to formalize my feelings into words and worship, so I sang:

"How beautiful are the woods on a fine spring day!
and how deeply green the pine tree where I worship!

The wild ducks' mating calls from out of the bottoms,
and the bobolinks praise Him for the season;

and the evening grosbeaks, brightly from the South,
for this morning praise Him. Am I so deafendumb

with such glad noises around me
I cannot find a song to praise Him with?

Kneel down. On bent knees worship Him
for ordering these woods; and greater praise

for then in His own image, mercifully
ordaining man to stand somewhere below Him, over all;

with sole right to know and privilege to become
one with the Genius of the Woods. Praise God."

The next day—Monday, March 16—I began my maple syruping, selecting from among hundreds of tall, straight maple trees as big at the base as a man, about forty to tap. I had help, in a manner of speaking, because the maple bush lay midway between Bobby Stringer's swampland and mine, and not only were Bobby and his little black dog there to meet me, but also, in accordance with the unfailing maxim that on a fine day people will materialize from nowhere to watch another man work, farmer McQueen from down the road had sauntered by also. Now, farmer McQueen and Bobby Stringer were both, to hear them talk, authorities on maple syruping. I was a novice. A full hour was spent instructing me on how high and deep to make the cut, at what angle to set the spigot, and how often to drain the pails. (I had borrowed from farmer McQueen's barnlot a huge flatpan he barely remembered having, and into this flatpan— four feet wide by eight feet long and six inches deep—the sap was to be poured. This flatpan was suspended over a trench, which I dug while the two men looked on and the dog, named Midnight, sniffed. Then, in the trench, under the pan, a fire was set—to be kept going until, as Bobby Stringer put it, "All th' s-s-sap b-biles down t' sweetness.")

While I was busy digging the trench, and chopping wood for the fire, Bobby Stringer and farmer McQueen debated the niceties of the spigots I'd already set. This led, by noon, to an argument between them, which led, in turn, to an inspection tour of each of the trees that were tapped: Midnight running ahead and peeing on the base of each tree, while the two men peered into each pail, dipped their fingers into the sap, licked their fingers, and argued. Even as I chopped wood I could hear them contend and countercontend as they moved from tree to tree:

MCQUEEN: Them with th' spoiled sides, they're not worth tappin'—don't run worth a hoot.
STRINGER: Well, l-l-lookit now, there's one, an' it's runnin' like a h-h-hurrah!

That, or something like it, and forty-odd variants on it, were their Ninety-five Theses that day; and, compiled and collated, might constitute a manifesto on the lost art of maple syruping.

At last we got the fire banked, the sap boiling, and a system for draining the pails. Farmer McQueen allowed as how it might work, Bobby agreed to look in on me from time to time, and they went home. As evening of the first day came on, and the frost began to settle, and the sap became sluggish, then stopped, I mused on how interrelated all Nature's workings were: how the sap in the trees and the blood in the body thicken and settle with cold; and how they thin and rise with spring, overflowing our buckets. As I trudged home that evening, bone-weary, the refrozen crust crunching beneath me, exposing here a dead mouse, there a leaf mold, and everywhere the half-decayed litter of winter, a doe bounded before me with morning freshness in her spring—she was just waking up, on her way to feed in the bottoms. I walked on home to my cabin; but, before going in, I paused at the door and said to the Genius of the Woods, who was also the Light of the World:

> Now, O Lord, let the night come,
> let the restful night come;
> and bring peace to all day creatures;
> and bring day to all night creatures.

On Saturday, April 4, I took another trip out. This time Lynn was with me, and we went to our landlord's place in Toronto, to take him some syrup. In the maple grove the sap was running in the trees and boiling in the flatpan. A long succession of warm days and cold nights—ideal for maple syruping—had guaranteed a good yield. Already I had bottled seventeen gallons of syrup (and several pounds of sugar, inadvertently left to boil beyond syrup), which I intended for barter. The maple-syruping crusade had been a success.

We left in the late afternoon, and it was our intention to be back the next morning, for church. The trees had been tended that day, night was coming, and we would be back before the buckets had filled. But all that evening—as we drove into Toronto, then visited with the landlord and his family, and then were put to bed there—the entire time I had a nagging sensation, more visceral than any conscious awareness, that the trees . . . the trees . . . the trees were bleeding, the sap was running out onto the ground, and there was nothing I or anyone could do—not catch, nor patch, nor quiet them . . . nor sleep, I could not sleep; it seemed to me that my own body was the tree, the wine of life spilled out onto the ground . . . and the night was warm, and the sap was running, and the trees were bleeding sap. . . .

We returned very early the next morning, sleepless and haggard, and as soon as I stepped into the maple bush my worst fears were confirmed: the smell of sap, sickly sweet, like that of a dead body; the wet marks down and around the trunks, as though each tree had peed itself; the buckets full and overflowing, and the spigots drip-drip-dripping. The hurt I felt, the physical constriction and mental anguish I experienced as I stood there—helpless, negligent, and alone—were incomparable to any sadness I had ever felt before, and certainly incommensurate with the plight of the trees. Had I returned to find them cut down, suddenly slain in the night by chain saws, I could not have felt worse. Then a man arrived in the clearing (he operated the telephone switchboard in Ivy) to tell me my mother had called, my father had died: his veins had collapsed in the night and been stripped, but to no avail. . . .

Lynn went down for the funeral, which was conducted, since my father had never attended church, by the Mexican radio preacher and faith healer who was one of my father's last clients. I stayed alone in the maple grove, tending my trees . . . wondering if, when the world's end came, it would come like sap in the night . . . trying to maintain, as I noticed new leaves in the maple tops, my conviction of resurrection. . . .

As I stood among the maple trees, it occurred to me that Easter was near. This would be my first Easter—a good time to join the Church. Perhaps Lynn would join with me. I hoped so. I had discovered the little cost at which one could live in the woods, but at what great price! High time it was to enter the world—which did not seem such a sinister prospect when I thought in terms of the Church and of serving Christ in the world. If what He'd said was true—"Be of good cheer, I have overcome the world!"—and if he did what he said he'd done, then there was nothing else to do; and if it wasn't, if he hadn't, then there was nothing at all.

I knew *I* wasn't ready yet to take on the world in His name, not even a little bit of the world, not even Little Rock. But God, like Nature, took time, and each task was sweet in its season. The time might come. . . . The time would come when, after children (three), and churches (five), and having become a Canadian citizen, I would return to Little Rock to face trial. Not for the first time, certainly, and not without fear and pain, the absolute Individual would face up to the absolute State, but not until after experience—of initial success, and subsequent failure; of community, and compromise—which would come with our first mission field.

For, having made my own peace with God, I was ready to act as an agent; and I took seriously Christ's great command, when He commissioned Apostles for every nation and sent them, by pairs, to every town where He himself would come, saying: "Start now, but remember, I am sending you out like lambs among wolves. Carry no purse, no haversack, no sandals. Salute no one on the road. Whatever house you go into, let your first words be, 'Peace to this house!' And if a man of peace lives there, your peace will go and rest on him; if not, it will come back to you."

But before setting out on a door-to-door, town-to-town campaign as a self-appointed missionary in an arbitrary apostolic succession (which leaped from Paul of Tarsus and John of Patmos to Blake of London and York of Little Rock),

Lynn said I should contact the Church. And Don Jay, the minister of Central United Church in Barrie, when I called said it was strange, but he had just had a call from United Church headquarters in Toronto, saying there was need for a student that summer to conduct a survey of a subdivision in Whitby, forty miles east of Toronto; the call had come through just moments before, and he was wondering how to contact me. It was then around 2:00 P.M. By late afternoon we had packed all our gear in Big Horse, bid a hasty adieu to the bush, and were off to our first mission field for the most energetic, charismatic, zealously prosecuted survey ever launched (under the auspices of the United Church of Canada, at least) on a sleepy suburb. While the several thousand unsuspecting souls whose fortune it was to dwell in North Whitby sat quietly at their dinner tables, or peaceably on their porches—reading newspapers and digesting their dinners, watching their children ride bikes or a neighbor water his lawn—as though that June 4 were like any other summer's evening; unmindful of the zeal that, like summer lightning, had been loosed upon them and would soon flash out among them.

A SPATE OF SUNDAYS

Seventeen

From where we lay in the bed of the truck that was parked on a hill in a thick copse of cedars, we could look down the slope past the apple orchard to the subdivision below: from Rosslyn Road, where the orchard stopped, south half a mile to the railroad track with the cannery beside it and the town beyond; east to Brock Street where the houses ended and farmers' fields began, and west to Cochrane Street, beyond which were woods and new houses under construction. The subdivision, comprising a gridwork of four crisscrossing streets and two crescents, had grass but not trees, and houses of two designs—those with doors opening from the right, and those with doors opening from the left, onto the concrete porches common to all. Certainly, from the distance at which we surveyed them, every house looked alike: the same red-and-yellow façades, the same picture windows looking out on the same squares of lawn, the same scenes taking place on Palmerston Avenue as on Centre Street or Donovan Crescent at the same time each day.

7:00–7:30 A.M.: Men coming out their front doors, entering cars parked in driveways to commute to work at GM in Oshawa or to factory jobs in Toronto. 8:30–9:00 A.M.: Children emerging singly or in groups from all but a very few houses, converging with children from neighboring houses, then with those from neighboring streets: walking, running, skipping, cavorting in a general throng toward the school that sits, surrounded by a playground, at the subdivision's west side. (A few teen-agers, book-burdened, bearing more somberly and at right angles to the general stream, cross the railroad tracks and slouch south toward the town high school.) 9:30 A.M.–noon: Preschool children outside their homes, on tricycles, trainer-wheel bikes, or grouped around pull toys, or studying holes they have dug or are digging; mothers sitting on porches watching toddlers, or pushing babies in strollers, or, as the sun climbs higher and beats down hotter on the treeless squares of brown lawn, sunbathing on towels in backyards. Noon: Schoolchildren come home for lunch. 1:00 P.M.: Schoolchildren leave homes for school. 1:30–3:00 P.M.: Little activity—most persons are at work, or at school, or inside. A few women hanging out wash. 3:30 P.M.: Palmerston Avenue Public School debouches its scholars, who wend their ways home along Palmerston, around Wardman and Donovan Crescents, up Centre, down Byron Street North, a few to Starr Avenue and Brock North and the old row of houses nearer the tracks (tarpaper or linoleum outside, all sizes, odd shapes), where one family of nine children who don't attend school have played together since early morning around an old tire hung from a lone weeping willow, in whose shade also an old amputee has sat in his wheelchair all day. 5:00–6:00 P.M.: Cars arriving, a steady stream up Brock North, crossing the railroad track, turning on Starr, turning on Palmerston, fanning out on the subdivision streets and crescents each to its own driveway, own house. 7:30 P.M.–dark: Families sitting on porches, men watering lawns, washing cars; broom hockey games in the streets, squads of bicyclists. Women on sidewalks calling children; men conversing in driveways. At the subdivision's south end, a train coupling, boxcars banging, the cannery whistle at nine—night shift. Further yet, the township of Whitby, church steeples, sunset. In the far distance, four or five miles, the dark expanse of Lake Ontario.

By day we lay on the high hillside watching the houses below; by night we slept in the truckbed—under the tarp which, on rainy nights, caught puddles of water and doused us. That was why we looked so scruffy the morning we sought out John Smith, minister of the Whitby "town" church, and the man Don Jay had said was to act as my supervisor. Dressed in jeans and bedraggled (it had rained that night), I with a stubble of beard and Lynn with disheveled hair, we had found the church (it was one of the steeples beyond the tracks) and gone straight to his office. He wasn't in yet, so we waited.

When he arrived between ten and eleven that morning, he assumed we were there to be married. He was a plump little man, middle-aged, bald, who shook hands heartily and spoke in a sonorous voice. His voice, whenever he spoke about anything relating to church, and especially to liturgical matters, took on a curious intonation, which I heard that day for the first time, but have heard often enough since to identify as "minister's manner": its main characteristics being an unnaturally unctuous tone delivered from as low in the bass register as the clergyman can comfortably manage; the responsive "ye-ess" (accompanied by slow nods of the head) interspersed regularly whenever a layman is speaking; and the burred *r* (which in Rev. Smith's case was reserved for the word "spirit"—in such a way as to render it not simply burred, as "spirrit," but clipped and burred, as

"spit-it" this word was Smith's specialty). More of his voice
we would get at church service, more of his handshakes at
parting.

"Come in, come in. Fine day, capital, a rain always settles
the dust," he intoned, indicating that we should be seated
while he scrutinized our clothes. He had been at the Whitby
church then for twelve years, going on twenty-five; and it
was his boast that, without ever visiting except by phone, he
knew every man, woman, and child, Catholic and Protestant, in Whitby township. Us he didn't know; *ergo*—

"And what brings you to Whitby today?"

When we told him, he was alarmed. He had heard nothing. There *had* been talk at the last presbytery meeting, but
no action taken, of that he was certain. He scrutinized us
again. Perhaps at the executive meeting he'd missed. If anything had been done, it shouldn't have been done without
him. North Whitby was part of Whitby. He trained in on
me. Was I a student at Emmanuel? What year? Hadn't
begun yet! This alarmed him the more. Wait, he said, he'd
clear this up, he'd call church headquarters in Toronto. And
while he was busy placing the call, where did we say we
were from?

"We're from Central United Church in Barrie," I said.

He nodded.

"You grew up there?"

"What does that matter?" I asked.

Rev. Smith reddened. His facial muscles tightened, and
the stubby little fingers of his hands clenched the telephone
receiver, bloodlessly.

"We grew up in the States," assuaged Lynn, "the southern
States."

At this announcement Smith looked even more discomfited.

"We immigrated here two years ago."

"Here?"

"Canada."

"But where in Canada? Where do you re*side*? Where are your *p*eople? And—I hesitate to pry, you understand, but— are you married?"

"This is our home now," Lynn said soothingly (while Rev. Smith said, scarcely audibly, "ye-ess," and nodded), "the Church is our family, and we've been married three years."

So John Smith, acting with more dispatch than was his habit, called Church headquarters in Toronto; and after frustrating talks with several secretaries and several sub-heads of boards, finally found somebody there who knew something about student mission field placements, and the North Whitby field in particular. He hung up the phone and faced us, solemn and fretful.

"The directive hasn't gone through yet," he said, in a con-strained voice; then, clenching his small hands together, "The board only met yesterday! Placements were only made yesterday. Perhaps for a while, until I get a letter, some no-tice . . . you would just—" He clenched and unclenched his fingers. "You'll be tired from your studies—no, you're not in seminary yet, I keep forgetting—well, you're probably tired from the trip."

"We're ready to start," I volunteered.

"If you could just show us the area," Lynn suggested, "so we'd know what it looked like."

This seemed a harmless enough proposition, a way to dis-charge his obligation and get rid of us at the same time. He acquiesced. Fifteen minutes later (it was now almost noon), having driven us around the subdivision and back to the church, he watched us get into our truck filled with sleeping bags, duffel bags, camping gear, tarp, and the idea struck him that, young and eager as we appeared to be, and equipped as we were for camping, and the weather promis-ing fair—

"There's a campsite just north of here, at Port Perry. Perhaps you could just . . . take a vacation. Come back and see me in a week or two; I should have something official by then."

We shook hands all around and parted, then drove directly back to the hill overlooking North Whitby, where near a ravine hidden by trees from the road we set up a more permanent camp: stones in a fire circle, a rick of cut and piled wood, the tarpaulin slung between trees. Then we backed up the truck between the trees and rigged our ground sheet as an awning, so that whenever the truck was parked we had a veranda for sheltering under, and whenever the truck was gone, and we with it, nothing of value was left. Lynn pulled from the bottom of our duffel bag a wrinkled seersucker suit—of the type worn in the southern States, cheap: thirty dollars from Sears—that I had not seen since college. She continued to rummage until she produced —presto!—her old faithful flatiron.

"It's not much," she said, holding it up in one hand. "But neither is this"—she held up the suit in the other. "But this old iron can work wonders. It got me through the school year, almost."

A wistfulness had crept into her voice. I had, after all, prevailed on her to give up her job before the term ended. It was still a sore point between us.

"Well, we're where the Church has sent us," I said, "and we're here as a team. Everything that's happened to get us here is not only past, but right."

"I know it's past. All I ask for the future—"

"From now on we'll do everything as a team. And we won't leave this place," I said (thinking that was the point of contention—the fact that we were always pulling up stakes, pushing on, packing, unpacking), "we won't leave until there's a church here" (with a sweep of my arm indicating the houses, which slowly baked in the sun). "Isn't that something worth doing?"

"Darling—"

"Yes?"

"If I should ever—not that I plan to, you understand—but if I should ever again—" Her voice trailed off.

"Should what?"

"Get another teaching job. Oh, I won't so long as we're busy here, starting a church and all. But if and when that time should come, here or wherever we go, all I ask is that you let me keep the job, not make me quit it—as you have twice now. Is that too much to ask?"

"Twice? When besides Barrie?"

"In North Carolina. The school year wasn't half through when we left; I had to say I had a rare disease, 'womb trouble,' which only a specialist in Ottawa could treat—in order to get my severance pay I said that. All I ask for the future—"

"I promise."

"Well, here's the flatiron."

We kissed, and while Lynn went off to build a fire and heat the iron and rig an ironing board on the truck fender, I set up a lookout post on the hill (like Jonathon Edwards' stile in the swamp) from which to brood over the souls of those on whom we were about to descend in power and a seersucker suit.

I remember the very first house, the very first person, we descended upon: 1026 Centre Street North, Dorothy Goodhand.

A fine June morning, and we had been up since sunrise. From my lookout on the hill I had watched and waited for the men to leave for work and the children for school, waiting impatiently for nine o'clock, feeling that earlier would betoken an excess of zeal . . . brooding one by one over each house on the first block of Centre Street North, while Lynn washed her hair and let down her hem so as not to appear dishabille. At last nine o'clock came, and we ventured on foot down the hill, through the orchard, across Rosslyn Road, and infiltrated the hostages' camp, the strategic northern front, the soon-to-be-liberated subdivision. We hadn't at that time devised a plan of attack. All we knew was that the woods were behind us, the world was before us, around us in unseen communion the martyrs and saints of all ages urging us on to augment their number with sentient creatures, living souls, and, who knew?—only God—whether this plump little woman at the edge of her driveway, watering her African violets, was destined since the world began to be one of the blessed? God only knew, not I, not even she until she was known and her name was called—and her name I didn't know yet.

"Excuse me, ma'am. We—"

She stood up and turned around to face me, and holding in one hand an African violet and in the other a watering can, peered at me through her glasses. I, already halfway up her drive, said, "Excuse me, ma'am. We—" with arms extended, indicating on the one hand Lynn, who was still lingering at the edge of the street, smiling, a little uncertain (this was the first house, after all), and with the other arm embracing the shining sun and all intermediate powers— "We're from the Church," I said.

Then, when she didn't respond visibly, just stood her ground, the African violet in one hand, the watering can in the other, as if waiting for some further announcement—

"We're from the *Church!*" I said, I fairly roared, "the *United* Church!" and began advancing on her.

Squinting at me through her glasses, she glanced furtively at the door, then at the steps, which were her only escape. Dropping her African violet, she lurched forward with a little squeal and broke into flight for the porch. I reached the base of the steps as the door banged behind her.

"Well," I said, my arms still extended, and looking around

at Lynn, who by this time was laughing, "well," I shrugged, "let's hit the next house"—which we did, and the next, and the next, and the next.

We canvassed the ten-hundred block of Centre Street North, and Wardman Crescent that morning; but we weren't very practiced in surveying yet, and we treated each call as an encounter and not as a job to collect data. (Later on we would refine our technique and crisscross our informants, until by the third or fourth callback we would know more about a household's religious history than any one member could tell us.) But for now we just knocked on doors, and said we came from the Church, the United Church, and were conducting a survey; and no one asked us of what, or to what end.

By the time we had canvassed the two streets and reached Shirley Sweet's house, we had some idea of what to expect from the world, which means we were ready for solace. Shirley Sweet was the first person in Whitby to receive us into her house and, probably, into her heart. People will receive strangers into their homes for a wilderness of reasons, and refuse them entrance for good reasons too; but nearly always their responses are based on old associations, former acquaintances, past encounters that in some detail resemble the present occasion. Seldom is a person found who is open to the present moment and responsive to the person knocking, without dragging last year's baggage and the next door's laundry into the bargain. When such a person receives you, as Shirley Sweet received us, the main promise of the Scriptures is fulfilled, for love will follow. And when several such persons are discovered living in the same neighborhood, and when they then discover one another—which requires one person's acting as a catalyst, at first—then the founding of a church is guaranteed, for the rest, all but the most brutalized and pinched in spirit will follow. As the Upanishads puts it: "When two persons come together, they fulfill each other's desires; so he who brings two persons together becomes a fulfiller of desires."

Not that Shirley, after she had had us in and fed us (I can't remember what, but I remember her remarking how thin we were), and told us of her husband, George, who worked at GM on "the line," and of her children, Blake and Melody, and how she and two or three other families (out of a thousand households in North Whitby) attended church downtown, at Rev. Smith's. (Had we met him? Yes.) Not that Shirley didn't wonder about us, especially after we'd told her we'd come from the woods and that I'd had a vision of Jesus; told it as briefly and nonchalantly as that, sitting in her living room, which was like every other living room we would sit in that summer, dark (in contrast to the light outside), cool (in contrast to the heat), with hardwood floors and colored drapes, a tile-surfaced kitchenette table and chairs, a sofa, a reclining chair, a print or two (from Woolco or Kresge) mounted on white plaster walls, and, blaring mindlessly from the room's corner, toward which all chairs were turned and all attention trained, a television. I asked her, I remember, to please switch off the TV, since she wasn't watching it anyway, and I, so long accustomed to silence, couldn't hear what she was saying. In such style, I, given an inch, took a mile, and our few highly charged words with the brooding silences between (for neither Lynn nor I were yet accustomed to small talk), coupled with the fact that we were clearly visiting every house "north of the tracks" with some unstated purpose in mind somehow related to churchwork—all this forewarned Shirley Sweet, ahead of anyone else, of the serious business afoot; for, as Swift says in his "Digression on the Use and Improvement of MADNESS in a Commonwealth,"

If we take a Survey of the greatest Actions that have been performed in the world, under the Influence of

Single Men; which are, The Establishment of New Em-
pires by Conquest; The Advance and Progress of New
Schemes in Philosophy; and the contriving, as well as
the propagating of New Religions: We shall find the
Authors of them all to have been Persons whose natural
Reason hath admitted great Revolutions from their
Dyet, their Education, the Prevalency of some certain
Temper, together with the particular Influence of Air
and Climate.

This description fit us to a tee, and Shirley Sweet, who had
dealt with her share of door-to-door salesmen, Jehovah's
Witnesses, Mormons, and Baptists of various ilks, who
worked part-time at the Shoprite cosmetics counter, and
who together with her husband had weathered the nine-
month-long general strike at GM, Shirley did not lack common sense, and the moment we left she called John Smith at
the church to report to him that she had "been visited" and
to ask him if we were "for real."

Smith was horrified. It suddenly occurred to him that we
hadn't gone to Port Perry, weren't off on vacation, and
might pose more of a problem for him than his three teen-
age daughters that summer. He had already spent the
equivalent of one premarriage counseling session (one hour
equals twenty-five dollars) on us, only to find out we were
married. Now the prospect of the two wild-looking "hippies"
who had breezed into his office, claiming to have come in
the name of the Church, the same Church he had served
faithfully (if quietly) these many years . . . the prospect of
them fomenting riot in the name of religion by knocking on
doors and calling on households in a part (a not very active
part, it was true, but a significant part, maybe someday an
affluent part) of *his* parish—why, it was outrageous! The
hasty decision to place a student (if such a decision had
been made) was only two days old; the selection of the student to be placed (if I, who was not yet a student, had been
selected) was the work of yesterday; while the parish

minister, the supervising pastor, the man most affected by
any decision concerning North Whitby, had not yet received
official notice or been alerted to notice forthcoming. This
was assuming too much! He was a servant, not a doormat!
The emolument of such slapdash doings in the Church—
which in the business world was called madness—was such
that were it not for men like him, John Smith, the world
would not only be deprived of its two great blessings, con-
quests and systems, but might even be reduced to the same
belief in things invisible. Churches would become bingo
parlors, and clergy would be abolished. What had happened
in Britain could happen in Canada too. Worst of all, because
most immediate, his uncertainty about us—about where we
were staying, what we were doing, what we were planning
to do—caused him the most acute worry. And he charged
Shirley Sweet with the task, should she ever see us again, to
tell us to contact him *immediately;* while he himself for the
second time in two days (the third time in twelve years)
took a drive through the subdivision, searching for us. But
by that time we were back on our hill, exulting over our first
day's encounters, drawing up charts of North Whitby (a
square for each house, a color for each persuasion: United
Church, red; Anglican, orange; Roman Catholic, yellow;
and so on), and brooding over the households destined for
the next day's visitation.

Eighteen

"The strange part was that, as a rule, when a stranger comes to your door, the first thing you think is, 'I wonder if my hair is all right'—that's the first thing an ordinary person thinks. But you came and said, 'We're Tom and Lynn York, we're here to visit for the Church,' and I thought, 'Well, if you do no more than the rest of them did, you never need come no more, 'cause them that's visited for the Church never left a brush on anybody.' Then the first thing I knew I was talking about Fergus, and him dead these many years, yet I'd never told no one how good he was and how much I missed him 'cause there was no one to tell. And the next thing I knew we were praying—I had this doctor's appointment for three-thirty, that's why my hair was up, and I thinking, 'I mustn't be late'—but it just seemed that the Savior was with us and that I had been waiting for this all my life and that now you'd come and you weren't going to go away, either. Then you were gone, and there was something I wanted to tell you, but I had to go to the doctor's. Then I spotted you going along up the street, walking from shade tree to shade tree, and your suit was all dark with sweat; and I stopped my car and motioned you over and told you if ever you wanted to hold a Bible study, you could hold it at my place. I was away a lot, but you could hold it there anyways. And when I said that, Tom didn't take it seriously; he said, 'You didn't stop to tell us that, you just wanted to let us see you all dressed up, and you look right pretty, Mrs. Curl.'"

Each day we were visiting, visiting, visiting: walking the streets and knocking on doors, finding housewives with their hair up in curlers, or with their swimsuit straps down, or with clothespins in their mouths. Lynn would come to the edge of the porch, while I went up to the door. I'd tell the woman who answered the door (for nearly always it was a woman) that we were conducting a survey for the United Church, and did she and her family attend any church? Occasionally we were asked in; more often not. As soon as I'd left a house, I'd mark in my notebook the names and ages of the children, the household's religious persuasion, and whether or not their church affiliation was active or nominal. Later that evening we'd color in squares on our master chart, on the lookout for a key house on each block from which to operate.

It was a block-by-block, beachhead-by-beachhead campaign, with desolate stretches and skirmish lines, and here and there a true battle. From our viewpoint each person was already churched, or potentially part of our church; no one was outside our dragnet; initially all were within. Reluctantly, and often only on the vouchers of neighbors, did we let people be what they were: RC or Ang., or Bapt.; everyone else was fair game. Roman Catholics accounted for roughly a third of those surveyed; another third was United

Church, with the remainder comprising everything else, from Seventh-day Adventist to professed atheist (the atheists were as rare as the Adventists, and were in some ways comparable). But it was the nominally United and the unchurched families (with the evangelicals operating as a fifth column) in whom we were most interested, their homes to which we returned most often, their number (perhaps fifteen hundred men, women, and children) from which we hoped to draw our fledgling church.

And just as we met a handful of saints, so we encountered some odd ones. (Though who, from a God's eye view, is odd? Or, rather, who is not?) Bill Rauchert, the neighborhood Noah, whom I found building, first in his basement, then in his backyard, a fifty-foot, concrete-hulled sailboat in which, like Sir Francis Drake, he intended to circumnavigate "the whole globe of th' earth." Always coming, never come, to church (though his children attended Sunday School); always building, never launching, his ark—was he afraid of the water? Finally, ten long years later, after the church had begun and flourished, then faltered and broke, and those who had been children in it, including his own, had left home, Bill Rauchert sold his house and set sail from Port Whitby, "a fugitive and a wanderer on the earth."

Or what of Bill DeGraaf? He and his sultry but brutalized wife of Dutch-Malaysian extraction were always foisting on us their nudist camp photos (they were "Mr. and Mrs. Nude Ontario," or some such title, that summer), trying to get us to join them for a weekend, a day, overnight. His fumbling attempts to gain sanction from us only frustrated him, for we were not affronted by his exhibitionism. We told him, when asked, that the tension his three daughters experienced between nudist camp weedends and weekdays at Palmerston School accounted for their poor grades; but we refused to regard his indulgence, which he imposed on his family, as sin. We ourselves had no awareness of sin, and why should one condemn in another what he does not feel in himself? I was a nature mystic, Lynn an anchoress, and if for the sake of the Gospel we were intolerant with ourselves, we were to that degree tolerant of others.

The propositions that Bill DeGraaf (and, on occasion, others) made to you, Lynn—attempts to sully, or at least try, the freshness you represented—you warded off as artlessly as the Virgin of Chartres warded off enemy archers. You simply failed to recognize, or refused to admit, that you had female parts, or were anything other than what we as a team aspired to be: androgynous agents of a spiritual force; not despisers of the flesh, but abstainers from its exploits. Not until Howard came by one morning (thinking there was choir practice, when there was only girl guides), and slowly unfastened your girl guide whistle, and held it in his hand, and held it for a long time, looking at you, then fastened it back again—not until then did you feel, as you told me later, suddenly naked; for in holding your whistle, he held you, and in fastening it back . . . but that was much later, and by that time we were locked in a love bond with Howard and Fran and so many others to such an extent that no moment's lapse or vagrant desire—not even the vivid, blood-rushing sense that someone you loved was aware of you sexually—could violate it. For of the Doners, certainly, as of Mrs. Curl, and Shirley Sweet (and the Rints, and the Bains, and the Grylls, and the Jacks), it would be true to say with the Quakers,

> I knew not that-of-God in me
> Until entwined with that-of-God in thee.

But this intimacy was not, as those who never knew Christian love imagine it, sexual; nor had it anything to do with bodies panting after other bodies, or minds afire for other minds as limited as their own. It was, instead, a love bond like an umbilical cord between each person and God; and the common experience of it, at that time, in that place, spelled community.

All this was a thousand visits and a hundred church services later. I mention it here to refute, not to prove, Swift's aspersion that "However Spiritual Intrigues begin, they generally conclude like all others; they may branch upwards toward Heaven, but the Root is in the Earth." Put any collection of human beings together, especially such a motley group as came to worship in Whitby, and they are bound to experience attraction and revulsion, differences of opinion, and petty quarrels. The wonder is that in two years of nearly constant contact among several hundred adults—in Bible studies, choir practices, congregational meetings, and committee meetings of all sorts: of elders, stewards, Sunday school teachers; meetings of the building committee, meetings of the board—the wonder is that there were so few squabbles, so much love. When dissension did arise, as it did at an elders' meeting over the issue of wine instead of grape juice, it was quashed with flair and dispatch: the elder in charge simply took half of the communion glasses to the tombstone maker's and had them sandblasted, and the congregation at the next Lord's Supper was given a choice between frosted glasses containing wine, or clear ones containing grape juice. Would that the split in the building committee could have been so easily solved, with one group proposing a splendid church in the round, and the other a small, standard structure; if only the two halves could have soldered their rift in one structure, chancel and nave. . . . But I am racing ahead of the summer lightning itself, which flashed in from the fields, raced through the streets at a mad enough pace, and spent itself in passionate preaching and praying, before it struck solidly and broke against a coalition of professional dullness and dug-in religion, represented from the first by Rev. Standpat himself, of the church

Holdfast, in the town Goslow, only forty miles east of the city Surefire, in which was the seminary Certain.

For Shirley Sweet had stopped us while we were out working the streets, and told us to contact John Smith. By this time he'd received official notice about us, and we'd been in town a full week. He, in a pet at our camping out, and worried about our surveying, offered to lend us some money (which we declined), and invited me to read Scripture in church (which I accepted). First, though, we were to attend church one Sunday and be formally introduced.

The introduction took place and, after church, when some of the elders asked where we were staying and discovered that we were camping, they prevailed on Mr. Smith to offer us the "old manse," a stately two-story building next door to the church, recently vacated since the Smiths had requested and now occupied a newly constructed ranch-style split-level house—the "new manse." We were to stay in the old manse until we received our first pay check. And while it had never occurred to us that we would get paid—for doing what? what the Gospel said do, and what we would have done anyway?—still, the manse we considered a boon. Lynn's first question was, "Where can I plant a garden?" and each morning, while I read in Greek the New Testament, she would work in her garden until 9:00 A.M., when we began our day's visiting. Over the six or eight weeks we stayed there, Lynn attracted on cool summer mornings the bums who made rounds of the churches for handouts and the children who later would form the core group of a vacation Bible school.

We were happy and comfortable in this old house. Even though it was furnitureless, and had been converted to Sunday school classrooms, it still represented an improvement over camping. The floors we slept on were dry, the stove we used was electric, and there was not just one bathroom, but two!—with such features as hot and cold running water, tile bathtub, flush commode, shower, and mirror—comforts enough, after two years of camping, to elicit from Lynn a surcharge of sensuous feeling. This posed a problem for me, for my energies were so sublimated and my purpose so focused that I had no time for such lapses and imposed celibacy on us both. The way I imposed it on Lynn was by taking her into the empty church early one morning and reading at her from the pulpit Malachi 2. How I twisted the purport of "Take heed to your spirit, and let none deal treacherously against the wife of his youth," to a jeremiad against marital sex, I find it hard now to fathom; except that I had not yet "had," as Rev. Smith never ceased to remind me, "theology." I certainly couldn't be trusted to interpret the Scripture (that is, to preach), but, liberal that he fancied himself, he was willing to risk letting me read it.

The Sunday in July drew near, as Sundays have a habit of doing, and while Lynn at the manse piano learned, so as to teach me, hymms (for we had had little exposure to church services, and were singing hymns for the first time), I practiced every morning—first in Hebrew, then in English—the Scripture John Smith had assigned me. On the morning of the fateful Sabbath itself, I practiced continuously from seven o'clock: first in the bathroom, then from the top of the stairs, and, finally, when the janitor unlocked the church at 9:00 A.M., from the pulpit. By ten-thirty, when people began to drift in from the warm summer day outside and to lethargically occupy pews, I was plunged in a deep trancelike muse, so much so that when John Smith took me into his study to robe himself and have quick prayer with the choir, the sound of his sonorous voice washed over me like running water, and I processioned (in seersucker suit replete with borrowed black gown) singing lustily the hymn Lynn had taught me, the top-of-my-head-hole filled with bright light, and my eyes all a-glitter.

John Smith opened the service, his resonant bass voice

calling all creatures, both great and small, to keep silence before the "Spit-it"—speaking, I noticed, into the microphone which, he had told me, I should speak into also, because the pews were wired for the benefit of parishioners who wore hearing aids. And, indeed, from my place on the raised podium I was confronted by an elderly, somnolent crowd—a few middle-aged couples here and there, with bored teen-agers in tow—the mean age around seventy. This first impression was reinforced by the spectacle of gawking, twitching, drowsing, staring invalids sprinkled throughout the pews—outpatients, Smith had told me beforehand, from the Whitby Mental Hospital.

One had a spastic tic in her facial muscles and a head that swiveled more than 180 degrees; another kept glancing compulsively at her watch and muttering loudly something about "time, time, it's time, time"; yet another kept getting up and leaving, then coming back and sitting down—so that, all in all, by the time the "approach" liturgy had been intoned, and I stood up to read the first Scripture, I faced, in Wesley's sense of the word, a "full summer church" that gave every appearance of having "a fair summer religion."

It was said of John Wesley that "he set himself on fire and let the people watch him burn." Thus did I that Sunday morning. In the first place, by the time I rose to read the Scripture, I had practiced it so often that I wasn't reading at all, I was reciting. Second, while John Smith had a deep bass voice, and I hadn't, he never projected, and I did. And third, the particular Scripture he had assigned lent itself to an oratorical treatment. (Prior to coming to Canada, I had won every high school oratorical contest offered, even propounding five minutes' worth of "I Speak for Democracy" to the U. S. Senate—which assemblage of worthies, together with the British House of Lords and the downtown Whitby congregation, must take the prize for somnolence.)

A prolonged silence preparatory to the delivery of the

Word (with a rustling of paper as the worshipers looked at their programs, while a lone voice mumbled "time, it's time"); then I opened the book and put my finger on "The book of the prophet Isaiah, chapter five, starting to read at verse twenty." All looked attentive, even the Whitby hospital patients.

Another long silence, then: "WOE UNTO THEM THAT CALL EVIL GOOD, AND GOOD EVIL: THAT PUT DARKNESS FOR LIGHT, AND LIGHT FOR DARKNESS: THAT PUT BITTER FOR SWEET, AND SWEET FOR BITTER!"

(A scramble on the front row to turn down hearing aids, which normally were let drone; a straightening of backs throughout the church, as those who had been lulled to sleep by Smith's voice were suddenly startled awake.)

"WOE UNTO THEM THAT ARE MIGHTY TO DRINK WINE, AND MEN OF STRENGTH TO MINGLE STRONG DRINK: WHICH JUSTIFY THE WICKED FOR REWARD, AND TAKE AWAY THE RIGHTEOUSNESS OF THE RIGHTEOUS FROM HIM!"

(At this broadside the middle-aged were perplexed, the teen-agers amused: not, certainly, at what was being said— no one paid attention to that—but at the unexpected force with which it was delivered. One or two persons looked around to see how others took it. One old retired minister in the front row, his hearing aid plugged in, sat with his clerical collar on and his eyes shut, nodding vigorously. But to these and other responses I was oblivious. I saw only Lynn, sitting midcenter; Lynn's gestures only I heeded—speak up, tone down, soften, speak up; and to Lynn only I spoke.)

". . . THEIR CARCASSES TORN IN THE MIDST OF THE STREETS. BUT FOR ALL THIS HIS ANGER IS NOT TURNED AWAY, BUT HIS HAND IS STRETCHED OUT STILL." (Accompanied by appropriate histrionics, enhanced by borrowed black robe.) "AND HE WILL LIFT

UP AN ENSIGN TO THE NATIONS FROM AFAR, AND WILL HISS UNTO THEM FROM THE END OF THE EARTH: AND, BEHOLD, THEY SHALL COME WITH SPEED SWIFTLY . . ."

(By now I had reached the midrun of the passage, and having spent the first part in getting the congregation's attention, I delivered the middle part in a low, rumbling voice, without breaking for breaths, like Ezra Pound's reading of his First Canto.)

"None shall be weary nor stumble among them; none shall slumber nor sleep; neither shall the girdle of their loins be loosed, nor the latchet of their shoes be broken:

"Whose arrows are sharp, and all their bows bent, their horses' hoofs shall be counted like flint, and their wheels like a whirlwind:

"Their roaring shall be like a lion, they shall roar like young lions . . ." (long-drawn-out from the base of the throat, each word delivered with power) "yea, they shall roar, and lay hold of the prey, and shall carry it away safe, and none shall deliver it. . . ."

(I was approaching the final verse now, one of my favorite verses in the Old Testament—I was tempted to give it in Hebrew, but resisted temptation; envisaged instead the dark cedar bush against which I used to inveigh, all alone but not lonely . . . above the howling of Bobby Stringer's dog and his distant moaning, amid the waning of winter light.)

"And in that day they shall roar against them like the roaring of the sea: and if one look unto the land, behold darkness and sorrow, and the light is darkened in the heavens thereof."

Amen. I sat down. Not a performance of which to be proud, for the very fact that it was a performance; but a good thing to have got through—one's first public reading of Scripture. John Smith and the choir carried on. . . . Afterward, it was remarked at the door, if not how well, then how loudly I had spoken, and that every word could be heard. From that day, if not from before, John Smith eyed me askance. I wasn't asked to read Scripture or preach until I took it on myself to preach (not in my own church, not yet, though that would come in the fall) in the Pentecostal Tabernacle on North Brock Street. When news that I'd done so reached Smith, he was forced by his elders to either give reason for not using me Sundays, or, by the end of summer and on a holiday weekend, to invite me to preach—which he did.

But by summer's end the movement afoot in North Whitby had reached what to him must have seemed alarming proportions. A neighborhood Bible study group had begun, with attendance rumored at near sixty persons. The downtown church's vacation Bible school, led in large part by Lynn and Joy Bain, a vivacious music teacher who lived in North Whitby, was drawing a surprisingly large contingent of children from "north of the tracks." An elderly couple from Smith's congregation, the Hares—he an elder, she a retired deaconess—enthusiastic over our work in North Whitby, and outraged at John Smith's lack of welcome to us, had left for an extended vacation in Florida and given us their house to live in, their garden to use, and their blessing on our efforts to create a new church in Whitby. And Don Jay and several other clergymen, none of them firebrands, who yet had faith in the guiding Spirit of God and were convinced of our sincere purpose, were pressing Oshawa Presbytery (under whose auspices the Whitby church came) to respond to the increasing demand of a growing number of people to form a new congregation.

For I had come through the apple trees between Bill DeGraaf's and Mrs. Curl's one hot July afternoon, having visited new houses all morning, and had looked in the direction of the tracks (the heat oppressive, and I tired and hot, and I hadn't eaten since morning), and seemed to have a vision of a girl walking along the dusty road. Her step was light and her carriage straight, lithe and supple her body; and though she wore a full skirt and her hair down to her waist, she moved smoothly through the heat which hung in waves. Then, without ever breaking stride, she glanced at me through the latticed branches of the apple trees, and smiled—her smile serene, her face and hair imbued with summer light—and passed serenely on and out of sight. And whether it was a vision of a girl, induced by the shimmering heat of the day and my own lightheadedness; or whether I saw a girl walking (for there were always children at play in the streets around the old houses, and the one old fellow without legs forever sitting in his wheelchair), I do not know and don't care. For that was the day I made one more visit, at a house I'd neglected till then, and met Mrs. Curl—she was then in her sixties—and saw in her the young girl, and she offered us the use of her home. Then began a series of moves to the homes of various parishioners, with whom we lived and in whose homes the church centered, Lynn and I staying for periods of at least two months each, over a span of two years, with no less than eight different families.

Nineteen

"There was an old lady who lived in a shoe, she had so many children . . ." describes Mrs. Curl's house in North Whitby, which, like the Abbess Hild's monastery in ancient Whitby, houseled such a brood of monks and misfits (at the height of our householding impulse that summer—counting outpatients, boarders, and friends—twenty-three; the usual number, eight to ten) that we were literally nearly stacked one on top of another, Lynn having to cook from the cot on which she slept in the narrow little kitchen upstairs, because there was no room to stand. The house wasn't large, though it wasn't small either . . . normal-sized, I should say, for a family of five; Mrs. Curl's had been a family of seven, but now she was alone and took in boarders—young men who worked at the cannery, single girls who stayed on, outpatients from the Whitby Hospital, and others. The normal tenure for a boarder at Mrs. Curl's, come he or she at whatever age, for whatever purpose, with whatever prospects ahead, averaged twelve to fifteen years. Even the boarder who lived in the four-foot-by-eight-foot closet in the basement (as distinct from the basement "apartment" of two tiny rooms, in which a whole family lived), even he who occupied this cell without windows, without light of any kind except what filtered in from the shared "bath" (a room bare except for a commode, a sunken drainpipe in the concrete floor's center, and, ominously protruding out of the concrete ceiling, a naked showerhead), even he stayed, emerging from his black hole only to work shifts and eat, fourteen years; while Gerty and Bob—she stone deaf, he the husband of her old age—had been living cramped into two tiny rooms without bath on the top floor for over a decade when we moved into the adjacent two rooms.

How Mrs. Curl managed to keep boarders we learned: it wasn't the comfort of living at 819 Byron Street North, in a frugally furnished, linoleum-floored, asbestos-sided, matchbox-like old house, filled new every morning at 7:00 A.M. with the noxious fumes from Gerty's chamberpot with which Bob, fat and filthy and lurching like a deckswab, descended the stairs (these morning smells intermingling with those from three jerry-built kitchens, two bathrooms, and the black hole below)—so it wasn't the comfort, nor the sweet smell, that made boarding at Mrs. Curl's a career project. And it wasn't the spaciousness—so many people cramped into such a waspnest, the cells partitioned from sight but not sound by plywood and even cardboard . . . with Gerty, stone deaf, shouting at Bob: her loud cackling voice, "DE-EAR, SWEET BOB, A-AT'S A PET!" followed by his low rumblings as he laboriously spelled out words of reply with a pencil stub on soiled scraps of paper. (She had outlived four husbands, and Bob had been her farmhand. Now she sat all day, her thick, gnarled hands and broad, bearded face intent on braiding her waist-length white hair:

sitting in the oversized bed draped with blankets and surrounded by cushions and swathed with wall hangings—this
padded cell with the queen-sized bed and the huge deaf
woman in it presided over by the oval framed visages of her
two dead parents, mighty-faced peasants and stern. In the
meantime Bob, her keeper, unshaved and unkempt, his dirty
shirt hanging out over his belly, which was hanging out over
his belt, sat all day in the tiny outer room, musing in silence
or scribbling notes in response to her deafening outbursts.)
So it wasn't the privacy, nor the commodious space. And it
wasn't the decor downstairs, either: the several artificial
flower arrangements (including a palm tree), and the
framed wedding pictures of Mrs. Curl's children, or the TV
fare that Mrs. Curl favored—Oral Roberts, Billy Graham,
Rex Humbard, and "Hee-Haw" . . . so it wasn't the interior
design or the entertainment, nor the creature comfort that
either provided; for neither provided much compared to
what we had come from—we who had walked on Persian
rugs in the woods. No, it wasn't the lodging that tethered us
to 819 Byron Street North; it was Mrs. Curl herself, she who
made us and everyone else feel at home, because she had
within what the world outside hadn't, and around her there
was what elsewhere there wasn't: peace. Not as the world
gave, gave she.

Every morning she would be up at 5:00 A.M. to do the
wash, work in the garden, and get breakfast, so that by the
time Bob descended the stairs with Gerty's chamberpot, and
the other boarders emerged from their nooks and crannies,
including the black hole downstairs, she not only had breakfast ready, but had infused the whole house with a spirit of
health and early-morning cheer. None of the boarders were
confined to their lairs, and no one felt constrained; for Mrs.
Curl's wasn't a boardinghouse, nor was she a landlady. It
was a commune, an abbey, a house set on a hill, a beacon of
light in a world subdivided, a home. And to any derelict

wreck who took shelter there, as well as to longer-term boarders, she was the mother superior *par excellence:* always cooking, washing, gardening, cleaning, yet in such a way as not to make the chore important, but the doing of it pleasant. She managed to involve everyone, not only in household tasks but also in the life of the family, which grew into a church, and of the church, which remained a family.

There was Norman, in his early twenties, who was raised at the Orillia home for retarded children, found work around Whitby for two years as a dishwasher, then left with a circus for the States. When I picked him up on Highway 401 hitchhiking out of Toronto, it was like picking up air. When I brought him home and gave him supper, then spent the night in the woods on the hill so that he could have my bed, Mrs. Curl was incensed and made room for him. For Norman the climax came when, after an abortive romance with Margaret, the cerebral palsied outpatient who homed at 819 Byron on weekends, and after weeks and months of attending church, he got by rote the Scripture verse John 3:16, and recited it to the assembled Sunday school. In Norman's own mind, he was reading it; and when reciting it he didn't stammer.

There was Fred, in his fifties, not really a bum, just one of the many unfortunates who everyone knows are around; of whom, when they drove past and saw him standing at the four corners downtown, doing nothing day after day, they thought not much, and not often. When Fred came home to dinner (a special: beef stroganoff) he thought it "sour, yer meat's gone bad"—which didn't endear him to Mrs. Curl, and she didn't invite him to stay. But since he put in time anyway at the four corners, a broom and bag were placed in his hands, and a cap on his head that said "Whitby." "What you doing, Fred?" "Workin' for th' city." On Sundays he rode his bicycle to church.

And what of the old woman with the buffalo robe? How did Mrs. Curl get her to church? "Well, it wasn't a question of getting her out, it was a question of getting her up. She had those fits, you remember, and when I went to her little tarpaper shack to visit her, that was when she was back from hospital after she'd fell on the stove and got scalded, she had this big bedsore on her back and the weight of this buffalo robe. It was the only cover she had. I was quilting convener for the church downtown and we had this quilt left over, for welfare it was, not for sale; so when they asked, 'Does anyone know someone who could use this quilt?' I said, 'I do.' And the ladies in the circle looked at me, and Mrs. Smith was there too, and they said, 'Does she belong to our church? She may need it, but does she belong?' That was when I gave up on the United Church, and quit going downtown."

And Art Holliday, who lived down the street, and who at the first Bible study at Mrs. Curl's, when a prayer had been said and the Scripture read and we went around the circle for comments, said: "I don't know enough about the Bible to say anything. But I hope I live long enough so that this young man can show me." Art Holliday, by profession of faith made a member of the church at age seventy-six, when they brought you into the emergency ward smashed and broken, your ribcage crushed and one lung pierced from the car accident, could you hear me as I read to you Isaiah 38—I who had never seen someone so mangled—and as I said to you "Thus says the Lord: I have heard your prayer, I have seen your tears; behold, I will add fifteen years to your life," did you nod? And did the shadow of the sundial turn for you, as for old Hezekiah, and are you living and leading worship still?

But what of Bill Jermyn, diabetic and blind and dying when we met him, dead now . . . who, after his wife had left him (and why not?), asked us to move in with him—

what of him? Though totally blind, he still ran a carpentry shop; though only in his late twenties, he sensed that he was dying; though dying, he was not religious. We moved in, and shifted to a vegetarian diet for his sake. We brought people in, and a West Indian doctor with whom I made hospital calls prescribed and arranged for him to visit Trinidad. With the doctor's wife as his escort, Bill toured the island; he even addressed a group of blind carpentry students. Then he came back, and died—but not until he had preached in our church on the text: "I was blind, now I see."

THESE ALL CAME TO CHURCH, who hadn't attended worship, some of them, since the little-church-in-the-wildwood: came, and continued to come; brought themselves, then brought others . . . Mrs. Curl collecting a carload of ladies who couldn't see, hear, or think—"To show whose side we're on"; with Louie Vickers in her buffalo robe (a sight for sore eyes indeed) phasing regularly to sacral time her epileptic fits; and Gerty declaiming in the midst of the sermon that, though she couldn't hear, "FEEL THE CLOSENESS, Bob?"; while Bob, in his dirty cotton workshirt and secondhand suit, slouched even farther down in his seat, and behind the broad brim of his old felt hat wrote Gerty a note that he did. And Bert, though he had the DTs, collecting each Sunday a ranchwagon load of Sunday school children from outside the subdivision; and Julian Beecroft, the eccentric inventor and head of the Unity movement, composing libretti for church-in-the-round; and the two Presbyterian ministers (visitors) exchanging astonished glances when one Sunday (in January) the Sunday school children processioned with palm fronds in their hands; and the Quaker commune who came as a body to ask, after the service was over, when the worship began; and the Baha'i missionaries who could scarcely believe they were invited to speak in a church; and the girls from Ontario Ladies' College (flushed, receptive), the Plymouth Brethren (stern), the folk singers (earnest, off-key), the teen-agers (enthused)—all came to the church which met in the school, came and continued to come. For Joy Bain, after vacation Bible school ended, had spent the rest of her summer devising a complete church-school curriculum in the hope of, and on the chance that, we would be able to get a church started. And Bill Grylls, Joy's father (he was then in charge of the school janitors), had badgered the school board until he was promised the use of Palmerston Avenue School on Sundays. For I had said to Joy, as she sat me down for an hour each day beside her at the piano, to teach me the hymns in the *Hymnary* and the responsorial psalms: "What will be the sign that we can start a church in North Whitby?"

AND SOME THERE BE WHICH HAVE NO MEMORIAL, and have become as though they were not: those who moved to escape community, or whose families have broken and scattered; whose heartiness was as the spring rain, and whose word like a summer shower; BUT THESE WERE MERCIFUL MEN, whose righteousness has not been forgotten . . . George Sweet making us a gift of his car, with a strike threatening at GM; Anne Budd, who taught five days a week, training Sunday school teachers the sixth, leading Sunday school on the seventh; Howard Doner having us (and the whole church) to dinner again and again; Dave Snoddy visiting his block for the church, though he worked sixteen hours a day and had been crippled from birth. Each responded as he or she was able, and some surprised even themselves as, seeing and being seen as sons and daughters of God, this motley group of incompatible people—some of whom had lived on the same street or crescent for years and had never spoken (except about each other, or behind each other's backs)—was drawn irreversibly into community . . . while I, with dogged zeal and drawn face, revisiting every house north of the tracks, divesting every person I met of his or her acquired traits, seeing in

each the One who was many but who remained One undivided—I managed to pass this perception ("Only God I
see") on; though, gradually, as time passed and I tired, a
reductive process set in whereby some, King Lear-like, were
stripped down to glory, while others, Macbeth-like, rose to
damnation. . . .

BUT THEIR CHILDREN ARE WITHIN THE COV-
ENANT, and they and their children and their children's
children shall sit in a circle and recall . . . all the intricacies
of blind remorse, the gropings toward God; the interrelations
between perfect strangers, the intermeshing of lives, the
showing, the probing, the ransacking of wounds; the saying,
publicly, of past shames and new secret vices, "I take no
pleasure in them"; the discovery for the seven times seven-
tieth time that the trifle of pleasure is not worth the tears of
repentance; and through it all the feet of brass, the robe of
flame, the wounded hands, the weary human face—all ex-
tending the light of the gospel a little farther into the darkness . . . before the darkness, sensing in its slumbering bulk
this kindling of conscious life, this brief and puny fire in the
night at which a few hundred derelicts gathered, rolled its
whale's back in the great flood, spewed, and submerged
. . . till universal darkness covered all. But not before the
far shore had been glimpsed, its shoreline of beaches and
coves, cliffs and anchorages, memorized, and the survivors
dispersed with the vivid imprint of what Christian community could be when, as Mrs. Curl put it, "The Savior was
there. If He hadn't been there, we wouldn't have seen Him."

There are three types of Christians, said Carl Jung: those
who have had a primordial religious experience; those who
have come under the tutelage of one who has had; and those
who subscribe to the Church principle. The Whitby church
members were, by and large, of the second variety, though
there were a few who simply shifted from downtown, and,
when the movement was over, shifted back. The movement

lasted two years, during which time the initial enthusiasm gradually crystallized into a formal liturgy; the congregation was rallied and then regimented into a United Church; and the inner life of prayer and Scripture study, which at first had found vent in experimental worship, virtually disappeared. One could graph this waning of spiritual intimacy (which corresponded to an increase in respectability) by the growth, and decline, of neighborhood Bible study groups in North Whitby.

The first Bible studies were at Mrs. Curl's—a small circle of elderly and earnest seekers after truth. There was little intellectual content in these sessions, and much prayer. The next series of Bible studies was held in Werner Kloke's basement, for the simple reason that Mrs. Curl's house was too small to hold the crowd. Still, the single-circle format was maintained, and from it leaders came forth. The assembly of sixty-odd who voted at a Bible study to constitute a church became that church's nucleus: Joy Bain, who played the piano and led hymn singing at the study, became the organist and choir director in the church; Werner Kloke, who helped conduct the Bible study, became the Sunday school superintendant; Bill Grylls, who arranged for Rev. Smith and two other clergymen to observe the vote, became the church's representative to presbytery; Peter Wiseman, inspector of public schools, who attended this and every other meeting with portfolio, became the chairman of the stewards; Art Holliday, who led in prayer, became the leader of the elders; Delmer Rints, time-study expert at GM (whereas most of the other men worked on the assembly line), became the church's treasurer; and so on. . . . After this meeting, and the "summit meeting" in Rev. Smith's office the next day between the clergymen and myself (a heart-attack atmosphere, with Rev. Smith clenching and unclenching his fists as he spoke of "the Spit-it present at the meeting last night; but what we have to ask ourselves is, 'Is it in the best interests of the Church as a whole to form a second church here in Whitby?'"), after this the Bible studies continued to grow in attendance, but to decline in "spit-it"—the zenith and nadir both being reached in the session held at Howard Doner, Sr.'s, mansion on the hill, at which a vitriolic dispute took place between the leader of the evangelicals, Werner Kloke, and the spokesman for the liberals, Howard Doner, Jr. After that the evangelicals decamped—for a time to the Sunday school, eventually to other churches—and left the liberals (who now dominated the board of stewards, the session of elders, the choir, and the United Church women's group) to form a middle- and upper-class United Church. Bible studies ceased altogether; and, except for a few pietists who continued to pray on their own and to lead prayer in church, prayer declined. With this decline of prayer, politics took over the various church boards and committees, relegating the free expression of spirit, like old Mrs. Vickers' fits, to church time. Gardenview United Church (for that was its name now) was beginning to resemble your everyday garden variety middle-class United Church.

A DECIMATION OF EASTERS

Twenty

In the spring of our second year in Whitby, when crows circled and cawed above the ravines, and red-and-white trilliums and jack-in-the-pulpits began to appear in the woods, I revisited the place on the hill where we'd camped overlooking the houses. Each of those houses was known to me now, each of the families within; and some—in the subdivision, Mrs. Curl's, Shirley Sweet's, Delmer Rints'; and off to the east, the Grylls' and the Doners'; and across the tracks, the Hares' and Bill Jermyn's—were as familiar as home. I could no more view the town as a whole, and without discrimination—as God, presumably, viewed it—than crows could turn white, or cease cawing. Yet to the casual view there sat the town as before—it hadn't moved, or been moved, at all. I knew that anything God did was forever, and that mighty works in Whitby had been done: lives changed, spirits lifted, energies released. But I myself felt depleted, as though virtue (if innocence be virtue) had passed from me.

Only the day before I had picked up a hitchhiker, and wished I were hitchhiking myself. I felt disoriented, jangled, the recipient of too much tea and cake; and my messages of late had turned from Jesus and his teachings (the man who had led us out into the light, onto a green hillside, and begun from the beginning: with a breaking of bread and a blessing on our hunger for love and warmth, and a little unfamiliar mercy in our lives), from his simple truths to the harsher demands of Bernard of Clairveaux, Francis of Assisi, Martin Luther—reformers and iconoclasts, advocates of change.

Now the presbytery, too, was threatening to replace me with an ordained minister. (Did they begrudge me my pittance of twenty-five dollars per week? No, it was to "free me" for studies—for all this time I was enrolled in seminary at the University of Toronto.) And even Bill Grylls, our representative at the presbytery—in whose house Lynn and I had lived, and at whose table we had eaten—had quit attending church after the St. Francis sermon and, not waiting for me to visit him, had visited me, and said: "Tom, you want us all to burn our houses, which we've been our whole lives building up. You want us all to set out on foot to the neighboring towns like Myrtle and Pickering, where our children and grandchildren live, and tell them to burn their houses and pack their goods. Then what? What more can we do than we've done? You're asking too much, I tell you. We were glad when you first came here, you and Lynn, and gathered us all together, and got us to start our own church in our own little corner, and we'll always be grateful to you. . . ." And in place of the Bible study, a building committee was being formed; and a minister who had bought a house in Whitby with an eye to retirement there, and who was a friend of John Smith's, was lobbying Presbytery to put him in charge of the North Whitby church.

I lay down on the damp earth that April day and gazed up at the blue sky. On maple and elm trees the branches were thick with new buds; the cawing of crows became distant and faint, then ceased altogether. Soon Easter would mark time again, time beyond time, in which one does not age any more than the spirit within, or the sunrise without, the person to whom Easter comes. Were one to live Easters only, he would outlive Methuselah, who outlived everyone except Enoch . . . were one to live only Easters. . . .

And lying at length between the earth and the sky, between the altar of earth on which man—whose flesh is grass, whose days are a tale told—is sacrificed over and over, and the blue sky above to which all that is sacrificed rises as incense . . . lying at length and in harmony, my valved heart with the earth's core, I meditated on Easter sunrises past, on Easter sunrises to come. . . . In a spring trance I marked time with Easters. . . .

Easter One had come, and would not come again; though spring and sap and Christ might return, the first Easter would not return . . . I standing among silent trees, maple trees, my father among cypress roots

> *(think now, as then, of the long*
> > *sleep*
> *the sleep of death,*
> *the bed of the grave,*
> *the mattress of worms,*
> *the coverlet of dust),*

progenitor of slime. . . .

And Easter Two: here, where Lynn and I first camped out overlooking North Whitby, sentineled with cedar trees and maple trees, the dark ravine below; four-thirty in the morning, a solemn little circle (Howard and Fran, and Murray and JoAnn, and Shirley Sweet, and Lynn, and the girl from Ontario Ladies' College where Lynn teaches, Susan). We stand at the edge of the swart ravine like monks and nuns of yore, invoking the first simple light, the first warming ray, the blessings of the new life; then sing a hymn and read a Scripture, link hands, and hallelu the rising sun. I want to kiss Susan—ritually: "trust men little, and religious men less" —so I kiss everyone but Howard, whom I embrace. Cold kiss of peace from Susan, her lips blue. Afterward all traipse to Howard and Fran's for breakfast, hot cross buns. . . .

And Easter Three: here too, but across the ravine, beneath the budding maple trees. Howard acting as lieutenant as each worshiper arrives in darkness. All wander off among the trees until the sun comes up. At the first commanding ray of light we come together, join hands, sing "Christ Is Risen Today." But between the act and the intention, the worship and the waiting in the woods, did anyone remember births? Were avatars abroad? Susan, "that dark job flitting among trees"—did she recall Diana Nemorensis, priestess of the wood? Lynn, who had stayed celibate against her passionate young will for two, for virtually four years—did Lynn rue secretly the circle and the crows as thick as priests? Then the circle of friends, surcharged with spring, dispersing like seeds on the world. . . .

Easter Four: Newmarket (as far north of Toronto as Whitby is east; and I still commuting to seminary, and Lynn to Whitby to teach), 5:00 A.M. with a teen-age group from the church, the portable church in which Lynn and I lived and where we held services Sundays. But Lynn is absent from the early-morning worship in the woods (the circle regrouped around the Mexican guitarist, and Jerry Olver, and teen-agers . . . and Susan from Ontario Ladies' College where Lynn taught, Susan again among trees . . .). Then the circle, like the Easter sun it worshiped, exploding, shedding spidery white light . . . like Jesus' love; and only by counting Easters can I not lose track of time, for time is a great lumbering beast running before me, and behind me stalks the hunter, also time; beside me, where Lynn should be, walking and talking, a corridor of black trees and blank night. Where is there to go but ahead? To turn back is repetitive folly, to turn aside a mistake. What to do but plunge into the thick dark ahead and hope the beast isn't lurking in ambush, and hope the hunter hasn't marked me for blood? Marking Easters my only hope now. . . .

Easter Five: Queen Charlotte Islands. I wear the stiff collar and clerical shirt of a padre to mining and logging camps, but over the clerical garb a sou'wester and an oilskin. A hurricane blows hundred-knot winds, rain lashes our faces, we stand pitifully beneath some bent-over trees overlooking the ocean as dark strands of rain connecting storm clouds above and heaving breakers below twist and funnel across the Pacific . . . no light visible . . . but we can see each other (not faces, but dark, huddled forms against a stark seascape), and there are five or six of us—enough. . . .

Easter Six: Bella-Bella, British Columbia. Again, the Pacific—misnomered, moody: no sun, no wind, no rain. We stand on the dock of the Indian village gazing across at Grave Island. Behind us the houses of suffocation, before us the house of the dead. Between the two, water; water beneath us. Each one is an island; all die. . . .

Easter Seven: Vancouver. Cyril Carpenter and I have flown down for his wife, Gloria's, death, and their baby's baptism. Cancer, and she is at home. We maintain vigil through Easter eve night, and perform the baptism at sun-

rise. Yellow her face, the sunrise was yellow (shining luridly in through the sickroom window), and bloated and yellow her belly. She dies that afternoon. . . .

Easter Eight: Yellowknife, Northwest Territories. It's 5:00 A.M. and cold (−50° F) as we trudge through the dark, which is never quite dark, from the mines on the shore of Great Slave Lake across the ice to the island of wind-shattered spruce and swept rock. Around the bleak island, a desert of ice; beneath the ice, permafrost. We crouch in a circle and wait for the eye of Jesus' love to fire our hearts. The guitarist freezes his fingers. The sound in the air as we sang "Christ Is Risen" was the puniest sound that ever had strength enough to die—the last song of the final huddle of doomed human beings on the edge of a vast, silent ocean. Outlandish and eerie, a cold sullen light, which was never quite light, filled the stasis—another day—and we trudged back across the desert of ice to the mines.

Easter . . . There must have been a ninth sunrise; there was. . . . But when was it? Where? I remember that too. I remember the cold, the Arctic cold. Earl walking before me over the rocks, in front, as an enemy walks; I behind him on the black rocks (the outcropped fault behind the warm house in which Lynn lies sentient, asleep) as though I'm stalking him, watching him as he watches the house, when it's I who am being ambushed. The sun rose, but so bloodless, so cold—a mock king without memory or heat—and no song, no silent prayer. (For what at the world's end is there to pray for but less heightened awareness, less time?)

Then the heat, the tropical heat. So Easter Ten must have been after the world was destroyed, and warming . . . before prostration set in, and stupor. And I alone running from ruin to ruin, a shatter of buildings my only defense against the monstrous God's eye outside. . . . I stop to lean in the shade of a wall, and a snake bites my hand; I lie in the dust amid rubble and brick, and spiders and scorpions sting me

. . . the musings of a heat-oppressed and paranoid mind.
But where? Where was the tenth Easter, the one lost to time
and in memory buried, blotted out from the book of life
—like the tenth man against the wall, shot; or the tenth let-
ter in a code, smudged; or the tenth daisy in a chain,
plucked—where was the tenth Easter and where was I . . .
when the sun and the light and the moon and the stars went
out, and the clouds returned after the rain; and the strong
men were bent, and the keepers of the house trembled, and
the doors on the street were shut; after the silver cord
snapped, and the golden bowl broke, and the pitcher was
broken at the fountain and the wheel at the cistern?

I lay seven years later on the same damp ground beneath
an even more darkening sky, listening for the cawing of
crows whose ancestors had been thick as priests; but no
birds called. A mock king, a false prophet, a failed visionary,
I lay as I had lain and tried to decide whether or not to return—to harassment, to judgment, to prison perhaps—and if
to return and to turn myself in was fight, or flight . . . marking time with springs, and springs by Easters, until I came
almost, but not quite, full circle to where I'd begun. . . .
But the cardinal number was missing, the terminal Easter
was lost, the circle of friends had dispersed on the world like
seeds, like slime, while I slept. And I said to myself as I slept
in the woods, remembering deaths and entrances that spring
in which Easter had died, "I will return to the house of my
mother, to the fleshpots of Egypt and ease"; but the
Preacher had said, "Live joyfully with the wife of your youth
all the days of your life, for all is vanity."

THE DRAGON AT BAY

Courthouse, 10:00 A.M., August 10, 1973

The courthouse fronts on Capitol Street, occupying an entire city block: gray stone, five stories, flags drooping from the arch—an old building, a characterless, colorless, rectangular government building. It is not the chief government building, because Capitol Street, on which the courthouse fronts, originates ten blocks west at the Capitol building—broader, domed, and garnished with more flags—because Little Rock is not merely the seat of the federal district, and the county seat of Pulaski County, but the capital of the state too, and boasts more and better buildings built with federal and state funds than its size (138,000) would warrant were there other cities, larger seats, in Arkansas. But the courthouse, which doubles as the post office and is called "the federal building," though not largest, and certainly not most striking architecturally, is the most functional, looks the most official, the most square and squat and solid of all the government buildings in Little Rock. It could almost be mistaken for the penitentiary which is not in Little Rock at all, but across the river in North Little Rock.

As you come in off Capitol Street you pass beneath the archway, with its drooping flags and heat-stricken pigeons; as you enter the paved inside of the post office floor of the building—cooler than the street outside, but not cool (98 degrees instead of 107 degrees) and pass the candy stand beside the elevator where the blind lady stares and listens to tell money with her fingers; and board the elevator, an ancient cage with a latticework door, operated by a black man in a uniform stamped "GS"; and ascend, slowly past the second floor, where the courtroom is located; past the third floor, where your father sat for twenty years, an internal revenuer (sitting in the same small office, at the same desk stamped "GS," beneath the same slow ceiling fan, above the same hot street—until he committed the grave error of treating Governor Faubus' income tax return like anybody else's, and got himself removed from the federal building on Capitol Street and from "Government Service" altogether), past all that, and on up to the fourth floor, where the U.S. marshal has his office and where, after all this time—all the years away in Canada—the cabins, the churches, the children—you are headed to turn yourself in ("ADVENTURER COMES BACK TO FACE CONSEQUENCES: Nine Years of Wandering May Cost Him His Freedom" the Arkansas *Democrat* headlines will read). And even though the FBI knows you are in town, they have agreed not to arrest you, if, as your lawyer has guaranteed, you will show up at 10 A.M. in the U.S. marshal's office and submit yourself to all the paraphernalia of American justice: arraignment, fingerprinting, plea, bond, surety, election of trial by judge or jury, or judge and jury, and its setting over to a date, October 11—when the weather turns cooler, the state's case

surer, till better traveling to . . . the blind lady who sits by
the elevator shaft, with mercy in one hand and money in the
other, while outside, in the reflector oven of a Little Rock
August, the pigeons ululate and defecate on the courthouse
pavement. . . .

Courtroom, 9:30 A.M., October 11, 1973

The courtroom is rectangular and gray—a miniature of the
building housing it—with windows on one side and doors to
a hallway on the other side and an entrance to the judge's
chambers at the rear. The judge has not come in yet, nor the
jury, but the court reporter and the U.S. marshal are present, and the gallery is packed. A low wooden fence with a
latchet gate divides the courtroom, separating the court
proper from the gallery, the chancel from the nave, as in a
church. You sit with your lawyer at the bar, a little table before you; at another table on the other side, the prosecutor
sits. You and the prosecutor do not face each other; both
face front, where in place of a pulpit resides the judge's
bench; in place of the cross, a flag. In the hallway, through
which those serving jury duty are being escorted into the
courtroom, there is some commotion, and there are U.S.
marshal's deputies at the two doors. Two more guards, in
uniform, stand talking at the rear of the gallery with two
plainclothes FBI agents. You know they are FBI agents because your mother identified them as the pair assigned to
her for the past five years. And now the door to the judge's
chambers opens, and into the courtroom comes the judge.
The court clerk announces that court in session. Everyone
stands.

The judge, a smallish, graying man in his midfifties, with
a short mustache, glances swiftly and judiciously about the
room, his eyes alighting on no one in particular—not you,
your lawyers, the prosecutor, the gallery (Lynn and your

mother are sitting prominently in the front row), the guards
—his glance surveying all. Then, with a sweeping motion, he
gathers his robes, he sits. The trial begins.

> THE COURT: We have for trial this morning 1964 Case
> No. 23, The United States of America against Thomas
> Lee York. Is the Government ready in that case?
> MR. RIDDICK: The Government is ready.
> THE COURT: What says the defendant? Is the defend-
> ant ready?
> MR. GITCHELL: The defendant is ready, Your Honor.
> THE COURT: You may call eighteen jurors, please.
> Members of the jury, as your names are called, please
> come into the box.

The names are called, and they come: through the latchet
gate that divides the courtroom—the gallery from the bar,
the audience from the actors—on their way to the jury box at
stage right. And as they come, shuffling or stalking past me
and my lawyer on their way to the tiered jury box, not one
of them looks at me, each stares straight ahead, each takes
his seat where the marshal shows him, then stares straight
ahead at the judge. Some are objected to and sent back,
more are called: women as well as men, blacks as well as
whites (though not so many women as men, and fewer
blacks than whites). Finally there are three women, one of
them black, and nine men, one of them black—twelve in all.
More were called than were chosen.

> THE COURT: The jury has been empaneled and sworn,
> the case will now proceed. Who is your first witness,
> gentlemen for the Government?
> MR. RIDDICK: Colonel Middleton Ray.

A thin, pale man in a quiet suit and tie with a large sheaf
of papers held close against his chest, Colonel Ray has the

precise and colorless air of a librarian. He bends stiffly at the waist to lift the latchet, steps through the gate and, half turning from the waist, latches it. As he walks unhurriedly toward the witness stand between the judge's platform and the jury box, the clerk steps out to meet him, Bible in hand. Very methodically the colonel transfers from his right hand to his left the sheaf of papers, raises his right hand, repeats, "I, Middleton Ray, swear to tell the truth, the whole truth, and nothing but the truth, so help me God," then switches the papers from his left to his right hand again, mounts the witness stand, executes a full turn, and sits down. The prosecutor, Mr. Riddick, stands up noisily, rummages through some papers, shoves them all aside, then crosses briskly to the witness stand.

Q.: Your name, please, sir, for the record.

A.: Lieutenant Colonel Middleton Ray, U. S. Marine Corps Reserve.

Q.: What is your present job or employment?

A.: I am acting state director of Selective Service for Arkansas.

Q.: Do you have custody of the records of the defendant, Thomas Lee York?

A.: I have his Selective Service file in hand.

MR. RIDDICK: I would like to offer this file, Your Honor—letters from the defendant York to his local board, and notices from the board to the defendant—as Government's exhibit.

THE COURT: Let it be received.

Q.: Now, Colonel, prior to the year 1963, the defendant York was classified 2-S, which is student deferment, and later his classification was changed to 1-A, which is the "ready to go" category. What was the reason for that change?

A.: The reason for the change in classification was the registrant's letter of February 10, 1963.

Q.: That letter is in the file?

A.: Yes, it is.

Q.: What did the letter say?

A.: Mr. York informed the local board that he was no longer a student at Duke University; and, being no longer a student, he was no longer entitled to student deferment.

Q.: Now, is that kind of change a matter of routine?

A.: Very routine.

Q.: Later on, the record indicates that a notice of delinquency was mailed to the defendant after he failed to appear for his physical examination. What was the purpose of that notice?

A.: The purpose of the notice was to inform the registrant that he was in violation of the Selective Service Act. The philosophy behind it was to give him the opportunity to bring himself into compliance. If he had contacted the local board, the normal procedure would have been to arrange for a second physical examination. And if he could successfully explain why he had failed to appear in the first place, the board might have removed his delinquency.

Q.: Was that done customarily? Was it a commonplace occurrence?

A.: Very common.

Q.: Now, in this case, we have a man who did not show up for his physical exam, and who did not contact the local board. Would you outline the procedure normally followed in such cases?

A.: He could be inducted. He could be inducted without the examination—

Q.: You indicated that the draft board, had he asked them to, could have given him another order for a physical?

A.: They could have, yes.

Q.: The law permitted them to?

A.: The law permitted them to.

Q.: Go ahead.

A.: He was then ordered for induction, with a mailing date of May 17, 1963, on the order.

Q.: Is there a record of that in the file?

A.: There is. We find an entry made that an induction order was mailed to him.

MR. RIDDICK: I think that's all.

THE COURT: Is there cross-examination, gentlemen?

My lawyer, Mr. Gitchell, stood up to cross-examine, but all the while, even as I heard the Selective Service director testify (dispassionately and impersonally, about routine administrative matters—for what could be more routine than a series of standardized forms, stamped "Clerk," and mailed by the thousands?), still, all the while he was talking, I was thinking about the tenth Easter—so much so that once, in the course of his questions, when my lawyer referred to "the defendant" and drew the judge's attention to me, the judge found me as Hippocrates found Democritus, "busy in cutting up several beasts to find out the cause of madness." It was all so strange, so passing strange, the sensation of being *on trial;* and to be in possession of all the facts (all but the last) and to be tried by those who knew none, not even the events leading to Easter One; then to sit through this laborious process of questions and answers, trial and error, in an attempt to ascertain—what? What else but the last, the lost Easter? Only it was unknown. I felt that if only I could remember that Easter, complete the series of which it was part, then the defense would become palpable, there would be no need to go on, and I would be like Democritus when Hippocrates asked him had he found the cause of his madness, able to laugh at a world that took him and his cutting up beasts seriously!

I tuned in for a moment to Colonel Ray's testimony: succinct and sane . . . logical, too, as Greek grammar. But it was as if they, with his aid, were puzzling alpha, while I was struggling to salvage omega. Colonel Ray, Colonel Ray, Colonel Middleton Ray . . . the name sounded vaguely familiar. . . . Could it be that he, who sat primly and answered like an archivist, had a file somewhere on the last Easter?

Q.: Now, referring to the file, Colonel Ray, can you tell the jury whether or not a notice of delinquency was ever sent to Mr. York at his parents' address?

MR. RIDDICK: I am going to object to the question as irrelevant.

THE COURT: The Court is going to let it go in.

A.: I see nothing in the file to indicate that it was sent to his parents' address.

Q.: The notice of delinquency was sent, rather, to what address? Can you determine that from the file?

A.: The difficulty I have in this case is that I cannot state definitely that it was not sent to another address, nor can I state definitely that it was. The only address that appears on the form was the address we just mentioned, the Ottawa address.

I tuned out again, thinking, "Easter One, Easter Two, Easter Three . . . Four, Five, Six, Seven, Eight, Nine. Nine better than none, ten better than nine, last as perfection is last . . . the series unfinished, the sentence unspoken, the choice of prison unknown. . . ." I admit I was scared; for suddenly it hit me (as it hadn't earlier), the full might of the United States: implicit in the judge's robes, the marshal's sideguns, the plainclothes agents at the door, the drooping flag, and the latchet gate . . . and I thought, "How did I ever get this far? Against the might of the state, and the ire of the South, how did I get away with it? And having got away, why did I come back—back to the United States, back to the South, back to Little Rock?" Then; "How does one come back to Little Rock?" and I remembered that too

. . . boarding the bus at Memphis: not wanting to get caught, yet wanting to; not intending to come back, but coming. Capable of reason, of turning around, of boarding the northbound: from Memphis to St. Louis, to Chicago, transfer there to Minneapolis, through customs (always trouble crossing the border, but not when heading North) and on to Winnipeg, then Edmonton, and finally Yellowknife —the end of the road, the gate to the North, the treeline of sanity . . . capable of reason, but not reasonable: definition of man . . . for even as I rehearsed in my mind the trip North, returning the way I'd just come, even then in the Memphis bus depot I thought: "or I could dog-leg down to Little Rock, a chance no one would recognize me if I avoided my mother's house, and even if they did they wouldn't care." That was the most depressing thought, that probably no one would recognize me, that even if they did they wouldn't care. After waiting ten long years so that they wouldn't recognize me, hoping now they would, thinking, "Maybe the FBI will be there waiting for me, maybe they will have gotten word from the border. Maybe it is not the United States' but the state line where they'll stop me, at the imaginary center of the Mississippi River bridge, flag down the bus, say, "Okay, this is where you get off, this is Arkansas. You were safe up there in that foreign country where nobody gives a damn, and even in them northern states where nobody gives a god-damn, but now you're entering Arkansas, you're treading southern ground."

. . . then working my way to the back of the bus, the sun just beginning to rise. Seventy-two hours I've been riding buses, seventy-two hours just to get to Memphis, and the sun just beginning to rise, its harsh light picking out the new boarders from the overnighters. The overnighters, all of them blacks, some of them servicemen, uncurl from their seats and wince at the light; while the new boarders, most of them white, all of them women, sit straight-backed and avid at the front of the bus, talking with one another. I stash my bag in the overhead rack and take a window seat two thirds back. . . .

. . . then crossing the Mississippi River, no roadblocks, no FBI, just muddy water streaked with sun and gray from industrial waste. Lining the bank on the Arkansas side are one-room shacks perched on stilts, bottomland. Then swamp and delta, cypress bottoms, shacks with mules, and fields. West Memphis: slum like East St. Louis, sump hole of the South. But a Howard Johnson's and a Holiday Inn front the highway—the cheery ladies in the front of the bus point to them: a convention could be held in West Memphis—backdropped by lifeless cotton fields and cypress swamps and tenant farms and flooded rice fields bordering the Cypress Junction bayou. . . .

Little Rock—127

So how do you come back to Little Rock? As to a convention, a Shriner's parade, a picnic. With your American Legion button, and your Selective Service card, your Social Security number, and your BankAmericard—back, back, past the Howard Johnson's and the Holiday Inn, past the lone mule, disk, and harrow in the baked brown field, the tenant shacks at quarter-mile intervals and the landlord's house at half-a-mile's remove, white and colonnaded, shaded by trees; past ten miles more of fields, red, raw, and tenant shacks, and swamp . . .

I tuned in for a moment to the trial. My lawyer was now developing the line of defense he had worked out beforehand—that the permanent mailing address I was accused of not giving was my parents' address, which I had, in fact, given—and there was some altercation going on.

THE COURT: Counsel, will you restate that question? I got lost.

MR. CEARLY: Yes, sir.

Q.: Colonel Ray, will you tell the jury what the mailing date was on the order to report for induction?

A.: The mailing date appears to be May 17, 1963.

Q.: Now, between the date when the defendant advised the board that his only permanent mailing address would be his parents' address, and the date of the order of induction—

MR. RIDDICK: Objection, if the Court please. That's a patent misstatement of the document. That is not what it says.

MR. CEARLY: Your Honor, I believe I quoted it correctly.

THE COURT: That is not precisely what it says. Counsel is at liberty to construe it that way, if he wishes. It is his theory of the case.

MR. CEARLY: May I read it, Your Honor?

THE COURT: It's his theory of the case. Yes, you may read it, if you wish to repeat it.

MR. RIDDICK: I'm going to object to piecemeal reading. I want him to include the phrase where York said, "nobody knows my address."

THE COURT: Well, you can repeat that part of it if you want to. Let's let counsel try his case in his own way. There are two sides, at least, in most controversies.

Q.: [Mr. Cearly continuing]: Will you read the last two paragraphs containing Mr. York's responses to that questionnaire?

A.: [Colonel Ray, reading]: "My wife I will deposit at a cabin approximately seventy-five miles south of Bathurst, my point of departure. More exact location would place it in the midst of the Serpentine Mountains. The Canadian National Railroad . . ."

It was embarrassing to hear the letter read in court. And if it sounded bad to me now, how must it have sounded then, to them? How must it sound to the jury? "The most foolish, proud boy in all of Arkansas," they must be thinking, "the most rash." I tuned out again and was back on the bus to Little Rock watching tenant farms with low-lying hills in the background, kudzu along the road banks, scrub oak and hickory and sweet gum with occasionally a lone pruned spruce reminding me of northern spruce forest.

Devalls Bluff

A single railroad track. A junction.

Exit—Stuttgart

Stock ponds dimpling the dry brown earth, grain elevators in the distance, more stock ponds. A sign: "Registered Polled Herefords"—white faces in green pastures, munching their fill—show cattle, tax-deductible. The land around all flat, flat, flat: riceland.

Little Rock—39

So tired my ankles ache, my temples throg, my nose runs. My eyes shut, but I catch myself: "My feet shall stand within thy gates, Jerusalem!" Light a cigarette, nose running so it wets the paper. I press my lips to hold the cigarette, it breaks, I wipe my nose—"I'm coming, Little Rock!" The smoke is hot, dry, acrid, burns my nostrils and my eyes. The musings of a heat-oppressed and paranoid mind, but in the end one always tells the truth. . . . Signs advertising motels in North Little Rock—where my cousin Sonny killed a black man, got two months . . . I'll make it. Lonoke, where I got picked up for speeding years ago . . .

Little Rock—10

Black slums and junked cars bordering a swamp, a high-rise in the distance, overpass. And now I see it—Little Rock! —two, three tall buildings, water towers, the state Capitol. The bus driver announces "Little Rock, Little Rock, Arkansas!" You blind old beautiful corrupt self-righteous city, you Jezebel of cities! I can't help it, I start crying. Hot tears roling down my cheeks blur all I see as the southbound bus rolls into Little Rock.

THE COURT: Is the defense ready to proceed now?
MR. GITCHELL: We are ready, Your Honor.
THE COURT: Call your witness.
MR. GITCHELL: Thomas York.

Off the bus as quickly as I can, I start walking down Main Street: the Wallace Building, where my father worked before the IRS moved to the federal building; the Marion Hotel, where he always lunched. And building after building—Haverty's, Gus Blass, Pfeifer's, the Arkansas *Gazette*, where I worked as a copy boy—names and places so familiar I feel like a child in Disneyland, in a dream landscape. Sunday morning and few people out; still I have the feeling everybody's staring at me, though no one knows me here. I know no one, except my mother, and no one here knows me. Davis is dead, the old black who did our yardwork, and Mary, his wife, my mammy, dead too; my father is dead— they all died here. I stop along the street to scribble this, I have to, and turn off Main Street onto Capitol, where past the federal building the state Capitol confronts me, and the posters for a movie called *Home from the Hill*. I stop again to write; it helps.

I really have to get some sleep, it's seventy-four hours . . . so I turn down Broadway toward the YMCA. The Broadway Bridge over the Arkansas River is beautiful in sunlight. At the "Y" I fill in the card while the black double-checks each item: name? address? Social Security number? Don't have one? He grins at me as if to say, "Who're you kidding, buddy?" At last, six bucks, and the key, Room 438, no elevators. Climbing up the stairs I think I'll faint. The heat so prostrating, the loud music from the open doors of rooms such an assault. It's Sunday morning and nine-thirty as I open Room 438—the heat blast nearly knocks me over. The room is radiator-heated, the window shut. As I open the window overlooking a tiled court, there are three dead pigeons on the roof.

Q.: (Mr. Gitchell, for the defense): Will you state your name, please.

A.: Thomas Lee York.

Q.: What is your occupation, sir?

A.: I am a minister of the United Church of Canada.

Q.: How long have you been engaged in your present occupation as a minister?

A.: Nine years.

Q.: Since 1964?

A.: Since June of '64; ordained since June of '67. I have had pastorates. I have been an active minister for eight years, and I've been on study leave for a year.

Q.: During the period of time from 1964 to 1967, before you were actually ordained as a minister, were you in a divinity school or some type of training?

A.: Three years' seminary at Emmanuel College, University of Toronto. At the same time I was a student minister, supposedly Sundays only, but it involved a great deal more than that, and I had two different suburban churches within fifty miles of Toronto.

THE COURT: What years are you referring to now, this three-year period?

MR. GITCHELL: 1964 through '67, Your Honor.

THE COURT: 1964 through '67?

THE WITNESS: That's right.

Q.: [Mr. Gitchell, continuing]: After you were ordained in 1967, what did you do?

A.: I then came under the agency of the mission board and was sent as a missionary for an obligatory two years; one year to the Queen Charlotte Islands, British Columbia, and the next year to Bella-Bella, British Columbia, where I stayed for an extra year. And, following that, I took a pastorate in Yellowknife, Northwest Territories. And from there, in '72, I went on study leave, after eight years.

Q.: Reverend York, in the fall of 1962, you were a student at Duke University, were you not?

A.: Yes.

Q.: And at the end of that year you left and moved to Canada, did you not?

A.: That is correct.

Q.: I would like to ask you about your decision to leave North Carolina and go to Canada. Without going into great detail, as I am sure you as a minister are inclined to do from time to time, try not to do that, but would you tell the jury what factors went into your decision to leave your graduate program at Duke University and move to the North Woods of Canada?

A.: Very simply, it was a compulsion. And not an external compulsion; it was an internal compulsion. I felt compelled to go to the bush. I didn't know why. It wasn't long before I was putting a religious interpretation on it. But, at that time, I didn't. I simply felt compelled to go. Now I can give the interpretation that I put on it afterward. But that was all tied up with having got to the bush, and having read the Bible and experienced a spiritual conversion. Then I understood things retrospectively. But at the time I had no idea why I had this tremendous urge to go North. It was a compulsion.

Q.: Was the avoidance of military service a factor in your decision?

A.: It was never the main factor—not consciously, anyway. And I do not feel, and I have not come to feel in years since, that—

MR. RIDDICK: I can't hear a word the witness is saying, Your Honor. If we wait until that truck outside passes—

THE COURT: Counsel, hold your examination until that truck has passed. And will the witness speak up, please?

Was it then and there, seeing your mother in the gallery, or was it earlier—languishing at the Little Rock "Y" and

avoiding her house and the neighborhood spies and the wire
taps the FBI had rigged her house with—when did the series
complete itself, the broken circuit connect, the lost Easter
surface . . . along with the reasons (deeper than simple
draft-dodgery, and darker than southern skulduggery, and
older than a single decade) for leaving it buried? Was it
then? For in trying to answer your lawyer's question, you
had to turn back, and delve down . . . and what you
dredged up startled you (though it had been lurking there
all along), appalled you . . . so was it then, on the witness
stand, at the precise moment a truck passed outside, that
you admitted to yourself that the truth, the whole truth, was
too deeply rooted and tangled for this or any law court to
cope with? Involved less with the military and the might of
the state than with the defiant pride of your mother . . . expecting you to be more of a man than your father, more like
her father, "Poppa," was: a self-made, driven, and rebellious
man, with his town house and his cotton plantation, his sawmill and his slaves . . . overseeing from horseback his gang
of black men who grubbed in his swamps and his fields,
lived in his shacks, ate his bread; mounting by night his
string of black women who picked cotton and kneaded
bread and rendered lard for him, wives and sisters of the
men he worked by day. . . . But how could I say that? That
it was a dead man, one run down by a Colonial Bread truck
in '39 on a street in Little Rock—dead before I was born—
who bequeathed to me along with his drive and defiance the
childless black woman who worked as my mammy (whose
husband did our yardwork) and who together with my
mother and my grandmother (in whose "town house" I
grew up) filled me with stories about my grandfather—"Mis-
tah Byrd," "Poppa," "P.A."—which would assure my never
taking seriously any human authority, not the judge of a
court, nor the governor of a state, nor the might of the

United States itself—knowing as I did that all power was passion and all strength was sullage and that my grandfather, who didn't need the country club because he had the country, who didn't need religion either because he was his own master, had possessed both power and passion, but not peace of mind.

I knew that because he had bequeathed, along with his frustrated blood and genes—and through my black mammy —his savagery to me; but I knew too, had figured out— somewhere, and at some time: whether in the "Y" that Sunday morning, or earlier, much earlier, as a child beneath the picture of him sitting on horseback, in his house—that his passion, and mine too, were inextricably entangled with the South; that cypress roots and black women and buzz saws and whips and horses were the landscape of the fury in our veins and of our mire; and that to get free of it, to transmute it (because it couldn't be expended: he had tried), I had had to go North—I knew that instinctively, had always known—to the hibernating, purifying snow. So that the whole trek North was nothing more (and nothing less) than a purifying rite, a repudiation. And having had to go, and having gone, now I could come back. Or could I? How do you come back to a place like Little Rock; and how do you face a jury of peers who have never left, never needed to, never stirred outside the country club, the church? But whether or not it is possible, or feasible, or credible, in the end one always tells the truth. . . .

Q.: I'll repeat that question: Was the avoidance of military service a factor in your decision to go north?

A.: No. It was deeper than that, it—

Q.: When you arrived in Canada, where did you settle?

The trial goes on, the questioning goes on, covering painstakingly the period of two winters: place names (Ottawa, Bartibog, Kingston, Utopia), dates (the day the mayflies came out, postmarks of the delinquency and induction notices)—all chronological, geographical, superficial information: Where were you at this time? When were you at that place? All in an attempt to establish that I really was in the woods for those two winters.

Q.: June of 1964; now we are well past the date of the alleged offenses. When you came out of Utopia, what did you do?

A.: I started more and more going into town, into Barrie, where my wife taught, and meditating in the park, and I entered the Church there. I went into the church in Barrie, Ontario, in much the same way we had gone to Canada, except by this time my mind was totally clear, totally empty. I went in and asked for the minister—I wasn't aware of the United Church of Canada as a denomination, but it really didn't matter to me what the denomination was—I told him I was ready to enter the ministry and join the Church. He thought maybe I had the order of things backward, so I joined the Church first and then entered the ministry.

Q.: I believe you brought us up to date on your subsequent career at the beginning of your testimony?

A.: I think so.

Q.: When did you first find out that you had been indicted by the grand jury?

A.: I think it was in 1969. I was in Bella-Bella, British Columbia, when I wrote the Selective Service board, so that would be '69. I received a reply from the U. S. Attorney's Department, stating that I had been under indictment since 1964. A copy of the warrant for arrest was in the letter.

MR. GITCHELL: Your witness.

THE COURT: The witness will remain in the stand, please.

MR. RIDDICK: My examination will be brief, Your Honor.

THE COURT: Proceed.

Q.: [Mr. Riddick, for the Government]: Now, Mr. York, in the summer of 1963 you and your wife were in the vicinity of Kingston, Ontario. Is that correct?

A.: Yes.

Q.: For about two months?

A.: Yes. I would say about six weeks.

Q.: And then you went to Barrie?

A.: Right.

Q.: And your wife taught at Barrie?

A.: Right.

Q.: What subject did she teach?

A.: I'm not sure. She would know. Ask her.

Q.: And you built a cabin?

A.: That's right.

Q.: On a concession? The seventh concession? Does that sound right?

A.: Sounds right, yes. And my mailing address then was Route 1, Utopia.

Q.: A small village?

A.: Very small.

Q.: Now, did you advise the draft board of your mailing address while you were at Kingston?

A.: No. I don't know that I had a mailing address at Kingston. I certainly didn't advise my draft board.

Q.: Did you correspond with your family, your parents?

A.: I don't remember. But I do remember calling my parents because my father was very ill then.

Q.: When did your father pass away?

A.: The following year, '64, and it must have been in April, because I was making maple syrup. My mother would know more precisely.

Q.: He died here in Little Rock, did he not?

A.: That's right.

Q.: Did you come home for his funeral?

A.: No, I didn't.

Q.: Were you in frequent contact with your mother during all this time?

A.: Yes.

Q.: By mail or by telephone?

A.: Both.

Q.: When you went to Canada, she lived where?

A.: On Garrison Road, out Highway 10.

Q.: After your father died, she moved to a house on North Grant Street, is that correct?

A.: Yes.

Q.: When was the first time you were ever in that house?

A.: This year, after I turned myself in.

Q.: You were not there earlier, when you first returned to the States?

A.: No.

Q.: Were you in Little Rock?

A.: I passed through Little Rock, yes, but I didn't stay at my mother's house.

Q.: Where did you stay?

A.: At the "Y."

Q.: When was that?

A.: Easter.

There it was, surfacing suddenly, surprising me far more than it surprised him . . . there it was, the lost, the decimated Easter: dredged up from slime, set back in time . . . completing the puzzle, perfecting the series, preternaturally present down to the last detail. . . .

. . . after an hour's sleep jarred awake by the blasts of a garbled newscast: "The gunman who . . . hostages hijacking . . . plea of not guilty. Los Angeles County sheriff's

. . ." Then a pop song, over and over by a chorus of black women:

> "Ah know-oh you'll sumday runaway,
>   but . . .
> That's why ah'll always luv you like ah do-oo."

The catch-phrase words and strident beat like live wires in your head . . . sit up in bed and hold your head and check your watch, ten-thirty; stumble down the hall to the latrine. . . . You're haggard, tired; the "Y" latrine filthy and hot . . . ten-thirty Sunday morning. After three days on the bus—a sequence of Good Fridays—suddenly in this juiceless place it's Easter, Easter Ten. Must go to church. Ask the minister to call my mother and invite her to his house. That way the FBI won't know I'm here. Not her church, Disciples of Christ too conservative, too patriotic; a Presbyterian church, more social activist. . . . I shaved and dressed, and went out on the street to hail a cab.

"We doan' keep up with white folks' churches," the cabbie said, "too many ub'm to keep up with, 'specially in that part a' town."

We were heading out Cantrell Road, past the drive-in movie, past the restaurant at the rear of which my father hung his shingle, too late, too sick, and too tired, past the Riverdale Country Club, up Cantrell Road to Kavanaugh, turn right: Pulaski Heights. The cabbie was right: churches, churches next to churches, churches facing churches. New, rich, half-a-million-dollar churches materialized on every corner—I had not known there were so many churches in the South. "This one will do," I said. I paid the cabbie and walked in just as the service was beginning.

The minister's thick southern drawl and the torpor of the organ didn't help, but the place was air-conditioned. The sermon was on Jonah and how he was three days in the whale's belly and Jesus three days in the earth, and how Jonah was a rebel and God loved everyone, especially rebels. I kept looking around the congregation for familiar faces, thought I saw some, wasn't sure . . . wasn't that Leif what's-his-name, who got Janet Ames pregnant? And Buddy Tackett, the athelete, whose first wife killed herself?

Then the service was over, and while the minister shook hands and drawled good mornings at the door, I malingered in the narthex. When my turn came, I asked if I could see him in his study. He scrutinized me, checked his watch, then nodded; I was conscious that I looked a little shoddy (wrinkled seersucker pants, no suit coat; short-sleeve shirt, no tie), but followed him across the thinly carpeted and moderately air-conditioned narthex into the cool, plush sanctum of his study, done in red. He left the door ajar, took his robe off, hung it, and remained standing. . . .

"I'm a Presbyterian minister," I faltered, "well, actually, I'm a United Church of Canada minister."

"Oh yes."

"But this is my hometown. I haven't been here for ten years, though; I've been in Canada. My mother lives here— Mrs. H. C. York?"

"Yes?"

He was fiftyish and florid, a large man. I felt small and sweaty. And smaller and sweatier I became as I broached my scheme to him, while he waxed redder and larger, responding with a fury he had not accorded Jonah.

"Why, do you know that sitting in that congregation this morning was Colonel Middleton Ray, head of the Selective Service heah? No doubt, ol' 'Stonewall' Ray would do anything to help you, anything he could, but you put him in a difficult position, you put me in a difficult position. Ah'll do everything for you that ah can, but first *get out of town!*"

I kept asking him if he would call my mother and arrange

a meeting for me. He kept asking me how old I was and confusing me with his own son.

"Ah understand, ah understand! Mah own son's goin' through just what you have. This town's tied that boy's guts around its fist. He won't come back. Ah just hope to Gawd he can survive it. Ah'm just glad you didn't go to your mother's minister; somethin's hurt that man real bad. He won't risk anything—why, he won't even join th' Ministerial Alliance. How old did you say you were?"

"Thirty-two, I'm thirty-two. Listen, won't you just call my mother? I don't see—"

"My own son's twenty-two. Psychiatrist said he had an 'authority problem'—authority of Gawd, authority of his father, authority of th' state—denies 'em all. Now he's bummin' around Boston because his sister lives there an' we can half support him without its lookin' like a handout. Won't write, call, anythin'—four yeahrs! Says th' pain in our faces is too much. Ah don't want to have a coronary an' leave him with that burden—"

By now he had me in his car and was driving me back to the "Y." I watched the streets of Little Rock go by while he ranted . . . the clean, white, prison-cell-like streets of Little Rock. Easter Sunday. A car passed, windows up and air conditioning on, a gray-haired woman driving. I bend down to lace my shoes, avert my face.

"Ah'd rather you jus' get out—fast!" he was ranting, "th' faster th' better. Ah'll put you on th' bus—you jus' get out, you heah? You leave your mother outa this; this is between you an' Uncle Sam. He might crucify you, he might let you go scot-free.

"Ah'll do all ah can for you, son, but"—he turned to face me, plead with me—"give me your word now, ah don't want to get perjured! Ah never saw you, understand? Ah never saw you, heah? Go on now, get out!"

I went up to my room and got my bag and walked out on the street. His car was gone. As though I'd never been here, as though Easter hadn't happened . . . these little omissions sent to try us. . . . Start walking down Broadway to the Broadway Bridge, turn right on Markham past the Robinson Auditorium and the Marion Hotel, to Main Street and the bus depot. As I enter, buy a ticket, and sit down to wait, from the jukebox ulaloos the wail of sirens, mocking—

> "Ah know-oh you'll sumday runaway,
>> but . . .
>> That's why ah'll always luv you like ah do-oo."

Q.: At any time when you talked to your mother, did she mention that she had been contacted by the FBI?

A.: Yes.

Q.: As a matter of fact, almost every time you talked to her, hadn't she been contacted by the FBI?

A.: Yes.

Q.: Your correspondence with various governmental agencies has all been typed. All on the same typewriter?

A.: I don't know. You could probably tell.

Q.: I probably could, if it turned out to be worth finding out. Did you take your typewriter with you when you went to Canada?

A.: Probably.

Q.: Did you have a typewriter with you in the bush?

A.: I think so.

Q.: Did you back-pack that? How far did you back-pack it?

A.: Not far. I think we probably left it at the first cabin.

Q.: I do pretty well with a load on my back, but I've never volunteered to carry a typewriter very far.

A.: There is such a thing as a cache—c-a-c-h-e.

Q.: I know that.

A.: So do I, and if I had a typewriter in the bush I would have cached it often.

Q.: At the first chance, I would think.

THE COURT: Let's move along, gentlemen.

MR. RIDDICK: I have nothing further.

THE COURT: Is there redirect?

MR. GITCHELL: I do have a few questions on redirect, Your Honor.

So was it then, or was it later, on the trip back? . . . the trip out of town longer, slower, the bus stopping at every little town—letting blacks off, picking blacks up, carrying slow-motion girls with vapid faces to Jonesboro, Judsonia, Blytheville. . . . This bus didn't leave the way the other had arrived, this bus was "St. Louey bound." Was it then while passing Beebe and your Aunt Inez's house, or the mixed farms outside McCrae, Searcy, Bald Knob—places you had visited with 4-H, FFA, recognizing and remembering suddenly the park where the girl like a goddess had kissed you and your blood welled up tumescent and you kissed her and she ran boldly, unabashed, like the farmgirl she always was, always would be, to the darkened fairground where the dairy cows were stalled (married and maimed in a car crash since, your mother had sent the news clipping); was it there, or passing a razorback hill, evening coming on now, the cool dark descending, stray wisps of cotton whispering in the furrows of last year, eighty miles outside Little Rock and a Hereford bull in an orchard like a king outcast, recalling the time when you hijacked the prize bull from the Arkansas Livestock Show, the night guard helping you and Tom Spradley and four more load the bull in the truck, recalling Spradley who had married Annabelle to avoid the draft and then joined the Marines to get away from her—was it then you realized that it was deeper than that? Than the military and the draft and your father dying of cancer? Was it then?

And what did it matter when it was? Because now you would come back, you would have to. Not for yourself, you had tried that already and it had proved a rout, a retreat; and not for the Church (the Church in the South—what a joke! what a mishmash of fears and flags, of platitudes and patriotism!); and if not for yourself or for the Church, then for what, or for whom? For your father (dead), for your mother (aging), for the girl you'd kissed in Searcy (married and maimed)? No, like everything else you'd done since Easter, that first Easter ten years ago, it would have to be . . . why? Why would you go back? If not for yourself, or for the cause, and least of all for the South—that soft underbelly, hog slaughter and harvest, that blind old sow that crushes her farrow and then gobbles them up . . . Then for what? For what? . . . For the simple reason that Little Rock was the one place on earth where, in order to understand fully, you needed to be understood; the one blind spot in your unified vision; the one bloodstain (and a deep wound, too, an old wound: unstanched, unransacked by Christ) in your stand-off struggle with Death. . . . So it wasn't scar tissue or phantom pain that called you back now, it was blood, instinct, the urge to know and the need to ask . . . to ask in the face of oncoming night, from the place where you stood as a child—of the Tommy Spradleys and the Janet Ameses and Buddy Tacketts: your jury—whether the light, the simple truth that we had all made mistakes, still shone in the darkness, or was buried in fatness, exiled in orchards, outcast. . . . I had asked myself, answered myself, as well as I could by myself; now it was their turn to be asked.

Q.: [Mr. Gitchell, for the defense]: Rev. York, have you ever used an alias?

A.: No.

Q.: Have you ever given a false address anywhere you've lived?

A.: No.

Q.: Have you ever refused to tell anyone where you were?

A.: No.

Q.: Have you ever instructed your mother, or any other person, to give a false address, or refuse to tell where you were, or give your address?

A.: No.

Q.: In your schooling, in your graduate program, or in your seminary program, or in anything, have you ever registered under an assumed name, or anything other than your real name?

A.: No.

Q.: Have you ever used a passport under a different name?

A.: No.

MR. GITCHELL: I have nothing further.

THE COURT: Is there rebuttal?

MR. RIDDICK: No, Your Honor.

THE COURT: Both sides rest?

MR. GITCHELL and MR. RIDDICK: Yes.

[Thereupon counsel for the parties approached the bench and conferred with the Court; the Court then addressed the jury:]

THE COURT: Members of the jury, the indictment returned by the grand jury contains two charges. In the first count it is charged that on or about May 1, 1963, in the Eastern District of Arkansas, the defendant, Thomas Lee York, unlawfully, willfully, and knowingly failed to perform a duty required of him under the Universal Military Training and Service Act, in that he neglected to keep his local Selective Service board advised of his current address where mail could reach him. The second count charges that on or about June 24, 1963, in the Eastern District of Arkansas, the defendant unlawfully, willfully and knowingly failed to perform a duty required of him under the Act, in that he neglected to comply with an order of his local board to report for and submit to induction into the Armed Forces of the United States.

The defendant has pleaded not guilty to both of these counts, and that plea on his part places upon the Government the burden of proving his guilt beyond a reasonable doubt. In order to find the defendant guilty, the jury need not be convinced of his guilt to an absolute certainty, but to what we call a moral certainty. To be convinced to a moral certainty is that state at which the jurors, after having considered the evidence and the instructions of the Court, have a firm and abiding conviction that the defendant is guilty, upon which conviction they would be willing to act without hesitation should the question arise in the more serious affairs of their own lives.

With regard to the first count of the indictment, the defendant has a continuing duty to furnish his address to his local board, and, of course, the board is entitled to rely upon the address given by the registrant. It is not material that the violation under consideration took place somewhat more than ten years ago, nor is it material that young men are not at present being drafted into the Armed Forces.

As to the second count of the indictment, the defendant contends that he never received the order to report for induction, if there was one, and, for that reason, says he cannot be held to have disobeyed the order willfully and knowingly. Let me caution you, however, that a person may act knowingly and willfully and thus violate the law, even though he acts from what he personally may consider to be good, or even lofty, motives.

I would remind you, also, that there has been a good deal of testimony about what the defendant did, what his wife did, and their movements and so on, after May and June of 1963. The defendant is not on trial for any acts that occurred after June 1963. Whatever you might think about what he has done or has not done since that time would not warrant you in convicting him of events that occurred in 1963. But it is proper for you to consider all the facts and circumstances both before and after the indictment period, in order to determine whether the defendant did what he did honestly and in good faith, or in knowing and willful violation of the Selective Service law. If you find that the defendant consciously and deliberately set out to disobey the draft law, or to fail or neglect or refuse to perform duties required of him under it, then you may find that he acted willfully and knowingly, even though he may have acted honestly, in his estimation, and with what he considered good motives.

I have caused to be prepared for your use a form of verdict, which reads: "We, the jury, find the defendant, Thomas Lee York, ——— as charged in the first count of the indictment, and ——— as charged in the second count of the indictment." You will insert in the respective blanks either the single word "guilty" or the two words "not guilty." Your verdicts need not be the same on the two counts, but, of course, all of you must agree. Your verdicts must be unanimous before you can return them to court.

Are there other requests or objections, gentlemen of counsel?

MR. RIDDICK: None on the part of the Government.

MR. GITCHELL: None, Your Honor.

THE COURT: The defendant may retire with the marshal. Let all persons in the gallery remain seated while the members of the jury retire.

[Thereupon, at 12:45 P.M., a recess was taken while awaiting action of the jury. At 2:10 P.M. the jury was brought into the courtoom, where the following proceedings occurred:]

THE COURT: Members of the jury, it is now midafternoon. The Court doesn't want to punish you and keep you without food. At the same time, I don't like to let the jury separate once deliberations have commenced. So I think I will ask the marshal to arrange to bring you box lunches and let you go on and work. It's raining outside anyway, and you don't want to go out and get wet.

I take it, at this point, that you have not agreed upon a verdict. Are you making some progress on either count?

THE FOREMAN: Some progress.

THE COURT: Well then, you may return with the marshal and continue deliberations. I think he has already ordered some lunch for you, and it will be here shortly. I don't know how long, but I would say, what? Fifteen or twenty minutes?

THE MARSHAL: About thirty minutes.

THE COURT: Thirty. The jury may retire with the marshal. The clerk will recess the Court.

[Thereupon, at 2:15 P.M., a recess was taken while awaiting action of the jury. At 3:48 P.M., the jury returned to the courtroom, where the following proceedings occurred:]

THE COURT: Members of the jury, have you agreed upon a verdict?

THE FOREMAN: We have, Your Honor.

THE COURT: You may hand it to the marshal, please. The marshal will hand the verdict to the clerk. The clerk will read the verdict.

THE CLERK [Reading]: "We, the jury, find the defendant, Thomas Lee York, *guilty* as charged in the first count of the indictment, and *not guilty* as charged in the second count of the indictment."

THE COURT: Members of the jury, are these your verdicts?

[*All jurors respond in the affirmative.*]

How did you feel when you heard the clerk reading, his eyes never glancing at you as he stressed the words "guilty" and "not guilty"? And how did you feel when the judge asked the jury, and the jurors sat straight-backed and solemn, then nodded—twelve heads on one neck? Then how did you feel when you heard the judge say . . .

THE COURT: The verdicts of guilty on the first count, and not guilty on the second count are received. I may say, though it doesn't make any difference to you at this point—and I probably wouldn't say it except that this is your last day of jury duty—the Court doesn't disagree with your verdicts. I think they're probably correct. It seems fairly clear that the defendant, whatever his motives, went to Canada and remained there for the purpose of evading service under the Selective Service Act. It's that simple. His motives, in the view of some, may have been good. They certainly were those held—or apparently were those held—by a good many others of his generation and time.

Did your mind balk? And did it balk at the verdict, or at the judge's gloss, or at the jury? Sitting all of them straight-backed and solemn, some of them sweating (the courtroom was hot, the day humid), some of them fidgeting, none of them looking at you or at each other, each staring dead ahead. Did you regard them, one by one, twelve in all, two tiers of discomfited people, waiting to be released from jury duty, sent home by the judge reassured? And staring at them as they stared ahead, did your mind, which had balked, frame the questions, did you ask—of them, of the judge, of the air: is this Little Rock? is this the South? are these twelve representative of it? And, having asked that, did you then ask the question you been waiting to ask all along, the question to which this trial was an answer, might have been, would have to be: are they, or am I, the true South, the South that colors all our dreams and drowns our visions? Did you ask it? Or did your mind balk, your spirit yield, did you too crave release?

THE COURT: The court will now proceed to sentencing. You might advise me, Mr. Riddick, of the defendant's prior criminal record.

MR. RIDDICK: I am sure he has none, Your Honor.

THE COURT: Has counsel for the defense any recommendation to make?

MR. GITCHELL: Your Honor, if I might respectfully suggest to the Court, I believe this is a case where a sentence of probation would be highly appropriate, for several reasons.

First, if the defendant were guilty of anything, it was a brief period of youthful carelessness, and certainly not a crime involving moral turpitude or active intent to violate a statute of the United States.

Second, if one of the reasons for incarceration was rehabilitation, the defendant's subsequent life demonstrates that no rehabilitation is needed.

The third reason is that the law under which Thomas York was convicted is no longer in existence. There could be, therefore, no deterrent effect in imprisoning him.

And last, since the defendent is gainfully employed and a contributing member of society, it would be a waste of his abilities, and a senseless drain on the state, to incarcerate him.

For these reasons, I respectfully submit that a sentence of probation would be appropriate in this case.

THE COURT: Thank you, Mr. Gitchell. Mr. Riddick, had the defendant been inducted into the Armed Forces of the United States at the time when he was scheduled to report, for what period of time would he have been inducted?

MR. RIDDICK: For approximately two years, give or take a few months.

THE COURT: Thank you. Gentlemen, your statements have been answered by the jury's verdict. As I stated before, it seems clear that the defendant left the United States of America and went to Canada for the purpose of avoiding military service. In this he was not alone; a good many others of his generation did the same. The defense has suggested that since the law is no longer in effect, and the danger of war not as great as it once was, the Court ought to grant amnesty. Now, after some of our periods of national emergency and some of our wars, I am told that we had amnesty. I have no objection if the Congress of the United States decides to forgive and forget all those people who, in the recent unpleasantness in Indo-China, saw fit not to honor their military obligations. I think the Court cannot do that.

And this brings us down to what I will call the final position, and that is that it will do no good to put Mr. York in prison. So far as Mr. York is concerned, that may well be true. I doubt that imprisonment is going to work any substantial change in his attitude. But so far as the law is concerned, it is still the public policy of this nation that violators of the Selective Service law have not been granted amnesty, and should not be. And failure to impose a prison sentence in this case would, in effect, be an announcement to all those, and I am told there are a number of them who are still in Canada and elsewhere, that they should come on home, that all is forgiven. This Court cannot grant amnesty.

Now, I have no wish to punish the defendant unduly. I note that he seems to have deep religious convictions. I hope that is true. If he does have them, and I assume that he does, they should be as comforting to him now as they have been in the past.

The Court suspects that if he's as good a man as he says he is, he will not have to serve much more than a third of his sentence. Had he gone into military service, he would have served something in the order of two years. It seems to me that the policy of the Courts in these cases ought to be to insist that a convicted defendant serve at least as much time as he would have served had he gone into the Armed Forces of the United States.

Accordingly, it is the judgment of the Court that the defendant shall be remanded to the custody of the Attorney General, to be by him imprisoned, on the indictment as a whole, in some institution of the Attorney General's choice for a period of three years.

Now, Mr. York, it is my duty to advise you at this time that you have a right to appeal, and that you perfect that appeal by giving a notice of appeal to the clerk of the Court within ten days from today. If you elect to appeal, your attorney doubtless will prepare the notice for you. If you wish to appeal and he does not prepare the notice, or you do not see fit to ask him, you may advise the clerk of the Court within ten days of your wish to appeal, and the clerk will prepare the notice for you.

You may go, in the custody of the marshal.

[Thereupon the sentencing proceedings in the case of *United States of America* v. *Thomas Lee York* were concluded.]

And it seemed as I stood before the judge, this jack-in-the-pulpit, looking down on me, I looking up at him; he sentencing me to three years' prison, I taking it without a word, without protest—all so passing strange. Was it for this I had returned to the South and submitted myself to the state? And what was this but a mock trial, a shabby pretense, what else but justice Little Rock style? The worst of it was the judge's saying he hoped I was religious, as though religion were synonymous with resignation, and I, if I was religious,

expected to behave, cause no trouble for the marshal, for the
guards . . . submit—because I was expected to, because I
was a Christian (for "Christian" substitute "sheep")—to
being overwhelmed by puny power and brief authority.
Why, take away the judge's robes, the marshal's gun—what
would you have? Two steers, not at all in prime condition,
two bleating wethers with the same lights, liver, and life
tackle as the prosecuting attorney, the defense counsel, the
jury—the jurors all sitting there sober-sided and straight-
backed, stuffed with box lunches, stifling yawns—fit for the
slaughter as I was. Could a naked courtroom be imagined?
A naked judge? An unarmed marshal? A prosecutor without
portfolio, a Selective Service director without files? But most
unimaginable of all a hung jury—just one person in twelve
concerned enough about what he was doing to sacrifice his
supper?

I studied the two tiers of faces: three women, nine men;
ten whites, two blacks; all adults and all Americans—my
unanimous jury of peers, attentive, waiting . . . to be
relieved of jury duty, to go home to supper. Not a juror certain about the verdicts, all hedging—passing the buck to the
judge. The judge reassures them, tells them they're right,
and passes the buck to Congress. Congress hedges, hems and
haws, passes the buck to . . . ? Not a soul in the gallery leaving the courtroom; everyone looking to me now, everyone
waiting, uncertain . . . And as the marshal approached to
haul me off, and the judge stood up to exit, I thought,
"Where has it gone? The certainty, the authority—even the
mistaken certainty of a lynching mob, the mad aplomb of a
hanging judge—what had it all come to? To a beaten man
beneath a drooping flag in a courtroom in Little Rock, Arkansas . . . to a panel of contestants chosen by lot and looking back, pillars of salt, all—pilloried as I would be if I let
them haul me to prison."

"Just a minute," I said.

The judge stopped, the marshal too, and the jury, roused from their torpor, looked up: some surprised, others impatient, all of them curious.

"I'm not going to prison, Your Honor."

The judge debated, for a moment, whether to say, 'Guard, seize that vain man!' But, secure in the power with which he was robed, and restrained by his moderate sense, he turned instead to address me:

"It is highly irregular, but the Court will recognize the defendant. Does the defendant have something to say?"

"Yes, sir, I do," I said. "We have since nine-thirty this morning been playing a game in which I was pawn. But it wasn't a fair game, because the power was all on your side. Surely you can't expect me, just because I played by your rules for a while, to pay the consequences of losing when there was nothing for me to win?"

At this point the marshal gestured, and one of his guards started for me, but the judge waved him back.

"I'm afraid I don't follow," the judge said. He spoke with tight-lipped restraint, and an effort at understanding. "Are you attempting to call into question the jurisdiction of this Court? I sincerely hope not, for that would, of course, constitute contempt—a serious offense—and it seems to me that having been convicted of one criminal act already . . ."

Now, certainly, was the time to back down, if I was going to back down, and go stoically off to prison; to give notice of appeal, if I was going to appeal, and fight the matter further legally. My attorney was pulling at my sleeve and whispering, "We'll file for appeal—appeal—appeal—"

> He's slippery as an eel—appeal—appeal
> We'll file for appeal—appeal—

But I paid my attorney no heed. It was all so strange, so passing strange, the whole scene. . . . I looked around the courtroom. There on the front row was my mother, shaking her head and yet pleased. Defiance of the might of the state —precisely what Poppa (her father), not Duke (my father), would do. She was weeping, yet proud! And knotted in a back corner some blacks, awaiting their time at justice Little Rock style; not wishing to appear too interested in what was happening in my case, but listening nonetheless . . . And then the jurors, stolid and severe for the most part, one or two of the women sympathetic, the men beginning to reflect the outrage of the marshal, of the mob . . . And Lynn, winsome Lynn, loyal Lynn, terrified for the outcome, assessing the features on everyone's faces to see what the outcome might be; there was Lynn, sitting midcenter, alert and responsive, ready at a nod to coach me—speak up, tone down, soften, now for the final pitch, the APPEAL! It struck me with the force of *déjà vu* that here was Lynn monitoring the crowd as congregation, waiting for me to preach; and here I sat, after all the approach liturgy and claptrap of dull ritual (the swearing on the Bible, the reading from the file, even the jurors' recess to box lunches), here I was with the Word that morning by morning had been given me, been promised me; the Word that had already hundreds of times been put in my mouth, Sunday after Sunday, each Sunday a little Easter (along with the command to not be afraid, to make no excuses at all): to tear up and knock down, to destroy and overthrow, to build and to plant nations and kingdoms. . . . I looked around the courtroom and saw only Lynn; Lynn's gestures only I heeded:

"What I have to say, Your Honor, is very simple, very plain, and not at all contemptuous, not at all vain. Only it hasn't been said yet, and I don't intend to be hauled off until it is said. It's just this. I appreciate the fact that all of you here have been hesitant about passing judgment. You, members of the jury, hedged on the verdict. You hedged on the sentence, Your Honor. But this was your time to decide.

It was your time, jury, to pass judgment—you passed it on to the judge. It was your time, sir, to pass sentence—you passed it on to the parole board and Congress. Now there's no one left to pass it on to, no one but me.

"All through the trial I kept asking myself, 'Who's to say? Who's to give judgment? Pass sentence?' And the conclusion I finally came to was, I am. Because I represent better than either of you the system that's failed here today. I stand before you as a child of that system; it is that system that has nurtured in me the self-certainty with which I stand here. I am better able to render a verdict than either of you, and I won't hedge on it either. It's this: I find the state guilty—of having neglected the weak and the poor entrusted to it, of having cheated and robbed the rest of the world; and of having murdered and exiled its own sons, and warped and spoiled its own daughters—its only hope for the future. Thus I sentence the citizens of the United States to imprisonment within their own cities, their own states, their own self-serving system—with all the fears and guilts and outrages that signal the ruin and collapse of this once great, but now derelict, nation."

The jurors, all suffering from heat, looked confused, choked with rage; the judge had withdrawn into smallness, a mute figurehead, a mere speck beneath a drooping flag. Only the marshal stood ready, waiting, hand on holster, watching the judge for the slightest motion, the slightest signal to seize me. . . .

"There's your verdict, your sentence. It's not me who's been on trial here today, it's the system. I would not go to war for such a system. I would not willingly return to live under such a system. And do you tell me that I should go to prison for a system I repudiate? I will not—the cost is just too high, the life too short, the craft and cunning of this Court too long to learn; the price too high, I will not—"

And while I was yet ranting, the marshal and the guards

and jurors all regarding me as soberly as judges, while the judge stared down in silence from his colonnaded sphere . . . I walked out of the painting as inadvertently as I had walked in, with the words, almost like a child's rhyme, or a mystic's mantra,

> *the life too short, the craft too long,*
> *the cost too high, I will not—*

on my lips. And the woman who, as I supposed, managed the gallery, and who had been behind me as I went in, but was now before me, the woman said,

"But darling! I believe you. It was never a consideration anyway. It's *much* too high. Too big, too—where would we put it? And late. The children are waiting. Come on."

"Oh," I said, "is it you?"

"Of course it's me, silly. Who else would it be? Who else would wait for you for over an hour while you maundered in front of a painting? If you can call that monstrosity a painting. It's more like—"

"What? What's it like? What do you see in it? Tell me."

"Oh, I don't know. It's too big, too big and too . . . impersonal."

And now it came to me, like the belated awareness of having walked through a door marked "No Exit" and wanted wildly to turn back (but where is there to go but ahead?), that the craft too long in the time too short at the cost too high was love. Hadn't I learned what love was from Mrs. Curl and my father and Lynn? And so many others: Peter Taylor and Father Murdock and old Harold Godin and the surly old trapper (whose name I never knew) and the sectionmen, especially Baptiste; and farmer Hooper and Mrs. Humphries, the librarian at Queen's University, and the girls—Fern DeCarle and Ruth Gavin—in prison; and Bobby Stringer, Don Jay, and my cigar-smoking angel (whose name I never knew, either); and the whole church at Whitby, so many—Howard Doner, Joy Bain, Bill Grylls, Shirley Sweet, Bill Jermyn, Norman, Bob, and Gerty, the Hares, the Klokes, the eight different families in whose homes we lived and at whose tables we ate, and Susan; and my mother; and through it all, Lynn—hadn't all of them taught me what love was? And what frame could contain my darkening vision but love? Not knowledge, certainly, for knowledge was partial and impersonal, and always a door beyond the door just entered stood unopened, into a room unknown. And not faith, for I had been through the gates, the gates through which I had to go, and had found my Jerusalem a city of darkness, a house of dust and dumb show. And not hope, for what was there to hope for but more time in which to learn better the craft, which was love? Only love, then, and only that which taught love was worth learning. Anything else was mere pastime, and for everything else time was past.

Lynn had turned around and was starting to leave. I reached out to take her hand.

"I'm going," she said. "The children are waiting, I'm going. What is it you want?"

"I'm coming," I said. "I just thought we'd . . . hold hands as we went."

"Hold hands? We've never held hands."

"Well, we can start. Unless you don't want to—"

"I didn't say I didn't want to." She paused, uncertainly. "You always called it 'foolishness.'"

"Well, let's start being foolish. Why not?"

Lynn looked indulgently at me, and just a little bit suspicious.

"Why all of a sudden? Well, it's too much to ask, it won't last," she said, taking my hand. "But if by some odd chance it should"—we were walking out the door now, our arms around each other's waists—"it will take a while to get used to, you understand."

"I understand."

We made our way out through the mall, past Teen Jeans and Woolco, into the dark and the cold outside, to the lotful of cars like dinosaurs idling, throbbing reptilian into the air within the druidical ring of high-rises, to where Stephen, our six-year-old, waited for us, playing with his new Yo-Yo.

With financial aid from the United Church of Canada, Thomas York appealed to the U. S. Appellate Court in St. Louis, and was acquitted on April 18, 1974.